My
JOURNAL
The Book of ME with Insights

Jason H. King

Order this book online at www.trafford.com
or email orders@trafford.com

Most Trafford titles are also available at major online book retailers.

Printed in the United States of America.

ISBN: 978-1-4669-1806-1 (sc)
ISBN: 978-1-4669-1805-4 (hc)
ISBN: 978-1-4669-1807-8 (e)

Library of Congress Control Number: 2012903688

Trafford rev. 03/21/2012

 www.trafford.com

North America & international
toll-free: 1 888 232 4444 (USA & Canada)
phone: 250 383 6864 ♦ fax: 812 355 4082

CONTENTS

ACKNOWLEDGEMENTS

First I must acknowledge my Grandmother who has prayed for me and has paved the way for me to be in this position. If it weren't for the Spirit working through my Grandmother I wouldn't be in this position of spreading this important message to the whole world.

Scriptures taken from the Good News Translations in Today's English Version-Second Edition Copyright 1992 by American Bible Society. Used by Permission.

Scripture Taken from the HOLY BIBLE, NEW INTERNATIONAL VERSION.

Copyright 1973, 1978,1984 by International Bible Society. Used by Permission of Zondervan Publishing House. All rights reserved.

Scripture quotations marked (NLT) are taken from the Holy Bible, New living Translation, copyright 1996, 2004, 2007 by Tyndale House Foundation. Used by permission of Tyndale House Publishers, Inc., Carol Stream Illinois 60188. All rights reserved.

DEDICATIONS

This is dedicated to me in all who feel downcast and ready to give up. I want all of me to remember that I, alone isn't never alone on this Journey while living on this earth, hope is Just a call away my brothers and sisters.

INTRODUCTION

My journal, The Book of ME with Insights is a collection of three books with a total of twelve chapters that contain life experience knowledge, wisdom, and the emotions of love, jealousy, joy, anger, hate and every day emotions you and I have to face to become better human beings while we live on this beautiful mother earth and most importantly the Father that is a part of us. We will talk about issues that we all face. This is every moment of our lives that we struggle with internally and externally in a world that is in a state of depression. We will journey through hard times, good times knowing that we are not alone in this battle. I know we can hold each other's hand during those times in the storms. Again, together we are going to journey on this emotional roller coaster ride. We are the ones who can make real changes by just knowing the world of peace is in all of me that am in you who are reading these words of hope. These words of wisdom will bring inspiration and understanding to the communities, work places, homes, and streets. We can truly know how to become productive sound living human beings. Revealing a more calmness in our facial expressions, body language, and having also the authority to clear the air of confusion intending to affect your spiritual man and the physical man. Without a doubt I know there are millions and even billions out there are willing to make a change despite There conditions, deep down the inner voice cries out for freedom, but I tell you readers there is hope and may you readers be a gift to someone very special as yourself. Amen. Now let's go!

My Journal, The Book Of Me With Insights

THIS IS A WORD TO ME (PART 1)

BOOK ONE, CHAPTER ONE

INTRODUCTION

This is a word to me living in all; these words through twelve chapters will be awakening. I know that it will live through generations; this is a word that can bring back life to the suffocating man and women who is struggling to live day by day with memories moving, stirring high and lower emotions now impacting the world outside of us. There is truly a war beginning inwardly manifesting from our eyes and limbs. All I can say is today is a new day. A joyous face can heal sending pure vibrant energies in a world that is starving for understanding, so to all of me who seek a word of healing to just get through hard times in this life without no one to talk to there is someone who hears, read, and feel your cries and pain in your soul. I know without a doubt there is hope at the end of the storm. Amen.

Let's go.

I can look to me for help,

But I also know I can become my own worst enemy.

Today I am just broken into pieces by one thought with strong emotions; This is not happy time

For me right about now,

For real! This mind has deep intentions to defeat me from the head first, heart all the way down to the toes and knees.

2. I have chosen not to live in fear; she's soul while I'm just the man possessing good cheerful energy that is my spirit man. I can accept my role in those moments of fear. Personally speaking I will not listen to those lies coming from me; truly this is a word to me.

3. Awful moments to me mean awful emotions have played a major role. This day I can stand recognizing that lowly beside must be put in place, I, alone cannot bring peace into the world without meekness walking on my side. Today while we breathe on top of the soils there are eyes looking upon one another with furious rage, uncontrollable with no knowledge of soul-excavation only disordered faces that's caged in their own concentration camps. Mentally leading the soul to a place where the rich man and his robe will live out memories.

4. I am positive whether I'm liked or disliked my palace is not made of earthly matter. This physical outer coat is just nature. I am truly spirit manifesting my characteristics to me that is also in you.

5. I have—or let me say, a part of me wants to cause this body we control to go into trembling and fear from the sole of the foot on up to the facial

looks, but through it all I am happy to know that I am able to stand by my side possessing real assurance thinking I don't have to become a victim to disorderly love. Lower emotions mixed with goodness casting spells giving out love potions leading souls downhill. We humans should know one erroneous move ruins good news. Now mother is singing the blues soothing and healing sick souls.

6. I have witnessed how she influenced my speech turning my ways into her ways, wasn't Jesus a poet-to-the-tree's out loud? she plays a major role with her minus touch, so what else can I do my news is now good news preparing my right hand to rule with soundness without minus ruler over my joyous mind and right hand. I am the man speaking healing all near and far, that's an Amen.

7. A Fearful thought with emotions has an unlimited appetite that is never full, saying, 'Enough is never enough,' this is a part of my persona that always hunger craving for more souls wearing the coat of flesh. Fear is her emotions in all of me intending to push me further into depression; it is the hope that is in me keeping me calm and under control. Reminding me that it is better to know my place than to be an emotional disturbed leader over cities and nations; to you readers reading about me

that live in you just remember <u>I am the left power house</u>. Maybe I do write in a way sometime that is more <u>mechanical</u> and less-loving soul rhythmic but my point is clear. I am more <u>positive</u>. I am just the opposite of her hand, raise the right hand in the air; finally you <u>see I am controlling this right arm and hand.</u> So now to you readers reading about my characteristics you can get a grip on life. Why? Because I have revealed to me my ways that is also yours now and forever and more, I am amen, say it with me. Amen!

8. I must continue by saying that we are in this <u>earthly vehicle</u> to figure out how we supposed to operate and function in this car body made of dirt, soil, ocean waters and then some. Thank heavens we have soul; truly, this is a word to me.

9. I have been looking for me for a long time, yeah, I know my place for real now but if I could go back in time, if I could I would, but it's the now I'm happy with today. I've had many problems and some deep personal issues that were emotional issues such as dealing with her ways and his ways. What I mean when I say his and her ways is the emotional characteristics in all of us human beings. Where? <u>Where resting beneath the crane.</u> It just happens myself the writer of this book was once lost and dominated by my own fear seated beside

me holding my courage hostage. Soul was there but not yet free from disorder recruiting taking me over with flesh movies occupying pictorial living beside beneath. Those days were reckless but today I can cherish all of me showing gentle soul and man. Today we have a chance to walk side by side on sidewalks with fewer issues and problems that will not affect our deep roots; truly, this is a word to me.

10. To you readers, I'm not intending to scare me, but the truth of the matter is when fearful thoughts come alive from within our heads. Fearful emotions run concurrent—I mean at the same time. Now we have allowed our hearts to be stirred up as well; I alone am less without my help-pure holding warmth, meekness, and gentleness.

11. I want me who am emotion in you to know and remember that I am the dominant one in speech. I know these words are bringing up emotions but the truth can make us free. We can feel the down fall of holding truth which can overcome a soul living in this body. That is not prepared to hold on when pain visits us. Pain is one of our helpers to keep our energy in balance, but do not take this word pain and began to bruise or hurt self. I beg me that lives in you not to do such things because once I've chosen to be spirit bound on earth. This

is now my creation and will be my home of my dreams. When the coat comes off me; that is only made of dirt. Than love and joy I'm hoping is our destination route. So let's keep hope alive. In the end there is a great reward.

12. We will talk on biblical things when we proceed to go down more than a hand full of scripts in my journal, the book of me, but for right now I want to us to know we can be better human beings no matter what outsiders think, regardless of pass errors. It's what we do today this very moment of our lives to those who have been given a second chance. Yes, my personality has been scarred by unhealthy spiritual order and by physical disturbed actions. I've always thought of myself as a champion. I felt I could release magic onto the world, but there was a great persona called fear that took me down to the lowest cell. A fear so deep it took the young nineteen year old I was and made me a walking horror movie. Dreams terrified me while every waking day I thought only sensual thoughts. Insecurity plagued me like the book of revelations. Today I am thankful to be one who is given a second chance to heal the world that is in me and in me who are reading these words of wisdom; truly, this is a word to me.

13. Sometimes I don't know what to say. It is her emotions living and moving me to become broken into little bits in pieces. My speech turns into liquid water. Soul is now unleashed awakening souls lock down mentally. There being freed from nightmarish cells. My love has shown me she's by my side whether I recognize or not. Personally I'm going to harmonize, for real, I am not playing.

14. I could not see myself in to the past, but today I am thankful to able to know the difference between my earthly worlds from my reasoning mind.

15. I can look to me and love me unconditionally; truly, this is a word to me.

16. I truly do love me with sincerity and honesty. My love is in all of me out there in the world who is reading these words this very moment. To all of me out there that speaks and wear different tones of skin color I just want to say I love me who am in you.

17. Music has influenced billions, millions of me seated beneath the crane for millenniums and centuries. I've been overcome by musical language resting beside me. I am in all who isn't music. I am just the spokesman being influence by her energy and spirit. Today music is still dominating

the airwaves around earthly connecting my power station with all of me around the world to become one in mind, heart, love, peace, joy, and soul; Truly this is a word to me.

18. Fear can take me away sort a like a category five hurricane; the truth is if where not aware of what's taking place I'm a find myself in harms pathway. It's not good to see innocent fall into hidden traps because of blindness of mind. Truly this is a word to me.

19. I just want to address to me that I can only be a positive role model. My emotions are good and courageous, joyful, uplifting, I'm the right hand man. the truth of the matter is I, alone can be overwhelmed and defeated by her—emotion if I do not recognize me, even the scripts speak on her-emotions saying, 'Then she said to him, "How can you say, 'I love you,' when you won't confide in me? This is the third time you have made a fool of me and haven't told me the secret of your great strength." With such nagging she prodded or urged him day by day until he was tired to death. So he told her everything. When Delilah saw that he had told her everything, she sent word to the rulers of the philistines, "come back once more; he has told me everything," so the rulers of the philistines returned with the silver in their hands.

Having put him to sleep on her lap, she called a man to shave off the seven braids of his hair, and so began to subdue him. And his strength left him." judges 16:15-19 NI V.

20. I have to speak the truth about what I felt deep down in a place where my soul lives. Monstrous emotions were triggered almost like a title wave or worse like tsunami. I tell myself the truth. If it weren't for me finding me I would probably be a walking nightmare and a danger to myself. Personally I can say that I am not covered and defeated by my lower energies that once held me in hell—excuse me if I have affected me out there that are reading these words in this book. Today I struggle but the lower world in me has no strong holds over my goodness.

21. Furious emotions burn in me but will not bring disorder to my character. It last for a moment then dissolves like an ice cube under the scorching hot sun, real talk. I'm my help in times of boiling points. I, alone is not my help, my help comes from my help-pure, my counselor, my lord who sits and walks beside me, together we work together to lower blood pressure, no need for doctors and medicine we like Michael Jordan and Scottie Pippen, unstoppable, the dynamic duo working to seal the deal and win it all, real talking.

22. I have experience every emotion from my lower self and the only thing I can do is stay in my place. I don't speak these words, I'm feeling me soul rush a title wave of woes, yes mam, no mam I can say no more, humility beats me down turning me into a soft man; not fighting with me it is only tough love, but I tell me the truth it feels like I'm getting the love of God straight through her-emotions. While his-emotions guide this mouth piece. Two become one harmonizing the spheres; truly this is a word to me, for real.

23. I love me enough to know it only takes one thought with lower vibes of negativity to set me back into depression. Today I can speak the good and the bad because deep down I have felt all wild emotions in me. There is nothing else to face, death of this body will not be the end of me, trust me. Though while still in this body it is my responsibility to speak carefully, this tongue and mouth can knock me down with no mercy avail, real talk. So I must know what I possess at all times and in my place at all times, I love me and I love me out there. Stay strong and know this is a word to me.

24. Right Spheres around the whole earth are dominating and overwhelming speech. It is also the other way around. man dominating effeminate language to show masculinity, today everybody

wants to marry one another but are unprepared when lower comes to represent self then man has no clue how to walk, talk, and be a gentle men. Truly this is a word to me.

25. I felt a sudden decline in motivation just for a moment, for real. A part of me said, "You are wasting your time so just give it up worthless, stick to your day job dummy." I'm telling me that is in you readers is that no matter what emotions where feeling together we can do ourselves a favor and examine me that is in all of you. Amen.

26. Music has the power to bring up memories with emotions running at the same time. These are the emotions of sorrow and joy, so get to know me.

27. I love me even when the world outside of me intends to harass me. I am with me no matter what the world says about me. This day I am holding on to hope and I am not falling victim to the god of these worldly snares.

28. There are moments weakness gets the best of my speech with lowly emotions.

29. Yes, I've made errors in my life that bruised and scarred my personality, but I have a choice to either get up or stay down. It's hard but I'm making the

choice to stand even though it hurts. One time I did intended to end me quickly sending me back to the soils of mother earth but mother spirit personality beside me I call humility overwhelmed me with warmth. Through all the fire I've been through I'm still upon this merciful mother earth; truly this is a word to me.

30.   I'm going to express my emotions to me, so to the reader if you don't agree or feel, I'm sorry, I can only express what lives in all of me around the earth who are wearing different skin; that is not what I am expressing me to. I am expressing me to soul beneath all the hardware, real talk; truly this is a word to me.

31.   I see those distorted faces, I'm not trouble, step on my toes I'm a hose me down with these words spewing out of me. I'm hurting, crying right about now deep inside.
Problem, you the one who failed the test! No mercy on you!

32.   Tears roll hard and fast down this face, my face as I pour out my pain and anguish. There is disorder all over the place, but I won't give in, I've been in the dark for seasons and didn't even know it. The world is cold sensual and calculating, so it is up to me to find my inner courts.

33. Once upon a time these eyes were confused and distorted descending straight to the lower cells with no mercy avail. Today this isn't my issue. I'm working and pressing forward to become a real good sound decision maker even when pressure is present.

34. I will not hurt me when error is present in my mind. Responsibility is mine while I'm alive and active physically. There are moments I am weak so don't be play and twirl with my emotions. Today I'm a face me even though it hurts, I'm a love me anyway!

35. No! I don't hide my emotions, there just under control. You hurt me and look down on me like I'm the problem and solver, yes I said it depression and anxiety wants to overcome me but I'm not buying it, yes I'm a recognize, but I'm not buying. I see me all day and can face me. Though I cry and sob deep down a part of me know what I need.

36. I know as long as I'm living in this flesh I'm going to battle spiritually, and that goes for all of me. No matter what color the skin or how intellectual the mind, spirit is-

Spirit and flesh is flesh. Today I just look out
At me and recognize that without
Meekness by my side I, alone is walking
Blind folded being easily manipulated by
The outer worldly things created by earthly
And devilish who is also mentioned as well
In the scripts overcoming leaders in high
Places. The scripts say, let his mind be
Changed from that of a man and let him be
Given the mind of an animal, till seven
Times pass by for him. All this happened to
King Nebuchadnezzar. Twelve months later,
As the king was walking on the roof of the
Royal palace of Babylon, he said, "Is not this
The great Babylon, I have built as the royal
Residence, by my mighty power and for the
The glory of my majesty?" these words
Were still on his lips when a voice came
From heaven, "This is what is decreed for
You, King Nebuchadnezzar: You're Royal
Authority has been taken from you. You
Will be driven away from people and will
Live with wild animals, you will eat grass
Like cattle. Seven times will pass by you
Until you acknowledge that the most high is
Sovereign over kingdoms of men and gives
Them to anyone he wishes."
Daniel 4:16; 28-33 NIV.

37. I am reprogrammed now living now embedded in love with joy. Though the Battle continues on I can recognize and see myself in the mirror. Loving what I'm seeing Knowing deep down I'm wearing beautiful well.

38. I see troubles and look straight in my face, you really think I'm a let me push me over, I see the edge but I'm not jumping, sometimes a part of me says, face me!

39. I see me all day and can face me though I cry and sob sometimes, but I know what I need and I'm going to get it, go after me not worrying about what disorder say about me. I'm a winner no need for the lotto, I have my own show time at the Apollo. Just another way of saying that joy is already in me. All alone at home with just one look in the mirror I can say honestly, I love me. That's as real as it gets, and no I'm not self-centered.

40. You think everything a game! This isn't play station. You lose here you're not coming back to the same body, there is no reset! Unless one resurrect you back to life.

41. Don't play with me deceive me you deceive your whole frame and body language, for real, yeah,

and if you who are reading about me don't accept me who is you, fear is lord over me.

42. It's a shame to see so many intellectuals fall victim to the worldly spectacles, and if I don't know check my doctor he'll take a look at the crane. Lazy, silly eaten hot dogs watching TV, small town, big city rented movies siting on my butt I can never recognize me with a bowl of frost flakes, a class of orange juice. These are the times, so wake up! Sleepy head life is too short here one minute gone the next minute. I like to hang around for a while so I can tell the next generation, so thankful to be alive I've would've been dead physically a long time ago; not once, not twice, not three times, not four, not five, not six, not seven, not eight, but nine times. One day when I'm gone these words will influence and help me that am living in young minds as well as older minds. To see my face that is also a part of me that is in you readers who are reading about me.

43. Millions Wish to have wings like an eagle and fly away from this reality, but the truth of the matter is truth will decide what the charge will be for hiding from her reality. mother spirit rest in all of me out there, souls reading these words has tap into her-emotions and didn't know what consumed them, saying, 'what in the world just

happened!' prison camps are filled with ME's speaking these words wearing mostly brown skin, but this goes for all of me no matter what skin tone, thank heavens for a second chance, Amen!

44. Yeah a part of me is the right sphere sending musical vibes across America, Africa, Haiti, India, South America and the list goes on as musical spews poetical language out of the tongue and mouth words of inspiration and awe—some ministry; truly this is a word to me.

45. A part of me says, 'Do you really want to lose your dream, your testimony, your life, and the insight possessing my house beneath the crane? I know you really don't so stop your complaining! And get up! I'm right beside you going nowhere. I'm your helper so don't hurt me again.'

46. I've learned a lesson and now I'm in love and knowing my place; Jesus expressed her—emotions, and because he expressed lowly emotions just like me we have a lot in common, don't know what color skin he was but it's his words that showed me in the scriptures that my life can change. He also demonstrated spirit man characteristics; now I'm in love with me that is in all with the four chambers, the heart. I now can say with my helper

beside that I love the soul within with all my heart, that's my only love, Amen.

47.　Deep down love knows my heart, my love now is soul deep, my passion is only for good and to redeem souls, my loyalty is forever and more.

48.　I've learned that if you can't accept the soul that is in you or cannot understand, distinguish and control emotions. Sensuality, fear, and uncontrollable anger will be ruler over you. Truth is if good cheer and hate is not distinguish everything you do can become drama, negativity, and hate, even a smile will look scary. Now you will in this state of mind become easy prey to the words of Jesus; Jesus words can now tear up your foundation from the roots up leaving you totally exposed and naked to the world. That's why every soul needs a mentor to help the weak to know the difference between his or her left hand from their right hand and not just leave them on their own, but to become a mentor and a leader. Jesus wanted his disciples to follow the spiritual positive energy not the flesh. The spirit is what moves the flesh and muscles. The flesh is only a vehicle for the spirit.

49.　He's the only gentle man that I'm going to express her-emotions too; in the night hours for real.

50. Deep down emotional wanted to fall in love, looking in all the wrong places, now emotional has finally found her-man. His name is Christ Jesus. Real talk we are married forever and more don't need know legal papers this thing is eternal, so if you readers want to know my spirit man you better first know your left emotional hand from your right soul recognize, Read his word, believe, rightly divide the word of truth, let the ocean waters refresh the soul, baptism, now walk it all the way out in boldness. Only the hungry can understand these words of wisdom, I'm a say Amen to that, why? That's real talk!

51. Listen, It must start with me if a change is for real. I'm the one who must figure me out, and Distractions are reigning over billions of me out there from small towns to big cities for real genuine. Soul that is me knows there is a right away; personally I'm not giving in to emotional confusion. no not this time around, I'm calling this love wrapped up, mixed up, shacked up with hate and joy, it's terrible towels being soaked in blood. Black young men and older men are being spiritually, emotionally dramatized and stagnant because of the lack of knowledge. Leaders, stereotypes, and front lines on the news personally my dreams were to become a professional basketball player; Michael Jordan was my inspiration back in

the eighties and nineties but the truth is this mind in me became stagnant because of lack of knowing who I was, so confused not able to distinguish my left hand from my right. I'll explain more on this later on. It really doesn't matter how talented or gifted I am because the mind must have balance and peace, real peace to function in a disturbed environment along with a confused system.

52.   Personally the environment didn't overcome me; I was my own worst enemy.

53.   This is the time for me to start looking at me, we need change and it must start with me.

54.   It's time to figure me out there are too many years I was down for the count, there is always a twelve count meaning I have a chance to get back up while the ref stop the count on ten. Close call I was ready throw all of me away until I heard a sound voice say, 'get up! Get up Jason! Because I'm with you always; this is one of my personal experiences of my life; August 22, 2005.

55.   I forgive me, now I can lift my head up with hope, no more will I give into my sleep and slumber giving devilish the keys to take hold of my joy and thunder.

56. Yeah, you think you know about me, if you knew the trouble and confusion I've been through I'm wondering can you endure the pain, fire, and brimstone. It's hot! I'm now striving to walk heavenly bound. Love isn't anything to play wit. I've treated me like shhhhhhhh be quiet, why should I, The world is in a mess, we walk around like mummies, yeah it's really sad to see that only a few souls are willing to stand and breathe taken the heat while the plastics melt right in front of all of me. The whole world is on my back every moment, every thought counts, me personally I'm not seeing me bounce to and fro. My soul is precious, soul majestic, prophetic, yup! I've learned to love me I said it. I do not doubt me this time around; surely paradise is soul real when I'm gone physically. I am a miracle some call me lyrical genius putting words together like two Lego pieces but I'm not feeding into, sometimes I've got to catch myself, I'm running over like the Niagara falls. Thanks for the compliments though, I'm one hundred percent loving me, yeah; it's me that is also in you who is reading these words of rhymes straight from the soul's inner room's. Nothing but love, too all my sister's, brother's, mother's, and father's, just want to let me know that lives in you hope is alive. know that where getting out of poverty, I'm coming straight from the heart with this one no other way I can express the flow of

God spewing rhythmic vibes of healing. I'm going to close this verse by saying, Amen.

57. There are too many Jonah's and Saul's but this book is My Journal, The Book of Me starring me created and written by me with God's mind to lead and guide, giving me authority. I am now the one who set fire without a lighter just a stroke of a big crystal blue pen on some paper now we just blow out of the mouth and tongue words of fire, souls hot. This is a lethal injection burning and scorching internal organs so just know I am not a menace, using mind to the best of my ability that's given me. I want me to remember that what I see in the mirror is in all heads, don't believe me just look at self in the mirror, and check out the face; arms, and legs, movements begin with us. I have no reason to lie or tell a story, I can go to my hometown and don't have to be on Maury show, soul is me, don't need to gratify finally standing on both feet for real. I am always on a spirit high; truly this is a word to me.

58. A part of me that is sensual wants the best of me, but not this time, I am truly balanced showing up through both eyes soundness. We see ourselves outside walking the streets looking very paranoid so sensually intellectually twisted. We don't have to walk in a trance blinded by fear. it's time to get

to know me; I am the problem solver my neighbor beside is a dreamer artistic holding imaginations, fascinations pulls the trigger of emotional me at the same time the heart responds, the right mind is a magic wand charming the whole world outside of me. The writer of My Journal, the Book of Me with Insights no more need for weapons of warfare I am the one overcoming storms and heat waves spewing out words in the mist of hurt. Tearing down the boards and creating work. This life in me is not a curse this time around; truly this is a word to me.

59. She is a part of me walking on the left hand side of me, soul emotional letting herself go, she is the feminine one manifesting her spirit through this frame we control. I just know without her I'm cold hearted with no soul and music spilling rhythmic news.

60. I am the reason seated, where? Beneath that dome of yours just call me Mr. Mechanical, The terminator, I'll be back. I am the kickstand the right hand man. Wherever I am I'm there speaking up for me against outer world enemies. Personally to speak up I better recognize gentle me seated besides holding soul and fire its energy.

61. I have no choice but to stand my ground when I'm being attack by silly ignorance intending to possess me with negative energies and spirit-lee.

62. Cheerful emotions are mine no matter what the ignorance in the world say about me. I'm holding the smile whether I'm accepted by the confused ME's or not. My job is to maintain my joy in the mist of the storms of this inner life and this outer world life. Soul is real and it isn't time to be timid dwelling in fear.

63. I must be honest to say that where there is a feeble mind there is a feeble hand. So know what I'm possessing or else I that am in you readers will continue to run to and fro bouncing around being dictated by fear day and night. We don't have to be defeated every day of our lives.

64. I know deep down where the soul resides there is some fight. It's time to separate the dark stormy clouds from the sun. Knowing the difference with eyes perfectly calm and sound seeing the way of holiness every step we take is bold with a side of finesse. This is the key to enter so we better first recognize, meek, and lowliness beside cheerful bliss that is now, later, tomorrow; truly this is a word to me.

65. These words are fire coals spewing out the mouth and tongue UN-caged paving the way, leaving minds on the outside in a pause and awe. Mother spirit is universal touching lives of all ages and gender. None of you men reading about me that is in you can stand without gentle and meekness by your side.

66. I have a temper that is furious and she steps in stirring up. There is now sizzle the mentalist is causing fires in wilderness, Ms. On his right hand side this is the reason for his sour looks, for real. Isn't responsibility a tick attracted to sour and good matter, mother and daddy I love me that is me. I can never forget myself who is reading about me without my help walking wherever I go, her soul is the opposite of cold, calculating, stiff-neck, and she is the emotion triggering dance and poetic vibe from big city to small town.

67. Here I am secure in me while discouragement is reigning as king over great cities and little towns. Truly this is the time to reach out to one another through our given abilities. Whether it is one, two, or three talents we all have that burning flame dwelling deep in soul. To all readers who loves to read these words of inspiration and insight. I want you to know that your journey in this life do not have to finish in confusion and hate, today I'm a

tell me that is you that your journey can end in peace and understanding gaining deep insight on race issues. I must speak on this for a moment because first of all I am black and beautiful, I know as a black human being I must struggle and reach down to the root, maybe down to the mantle of the earth to succeed; I've learned and have come to the conclusion that I am the soul; the helper; the musician, the artist, the lowly and the meekness walking the earth; man alone is not a gentle men without her-emotions. I've been in ignorance of me for two and a half decades now wearing the scars of past mistakes that has bruised my personality, but I am not a product of my environment. I am today a disciple for Christ Jesus the only man in my life that I will be loyal too. He's my man! And you readers can call me whatever you want because deep in soul I'm secure possessing soul juice, ecstatic forever and more, I'm either with me or against me. I'm not even on stage yet I'm just blown away by the nuclear explosion with the mouth wide open. This is coast to coast am, the end of times is the end of earthly me, hearing me is like a call to battle. Drunks sober up religious fanatics are addicts and can't even grasp me living in all of me seeking and hungering. I'm a stand by my side to the end of me. Fear is not overwhelming me this time around I'm prepared, even though fear is running wild for miles I know no hell formed against me can bear to look at me; truly this is a word to me.

68. I remember the time me and my two sisters was messing around with a Ouija board it didn't scare the shoes off me but it did made me think of the spirit world a whole lot more. Even to this day I think back way deep into the mind. I alone didn't know any better. Man has messed around and disfigured his soul, his role is confusion mixed with a minus look that isn't healthy. Personally I think he's on a journey of discovery to find missing treasures, he don't even realize it is already in him writing stories is just one of his abilities. While she is singing herself back to love in moments of harmony.

69. As a youngster effeminate and masculine was getting the best of one another, and when I say the best these emotions had me feeling like I was in a spiritual cocoon or better yet a prisoner of my own self. Fear was winning causing scary movies to be played in my soul twenty four seven. I became the enemy to earth while walking the earth and didn't know what devilish emotions meant until the inner voice called me back to Mother dears house in Opp, Alabama August 17, 1998 one day before my 18th Birthday.

70. I've made some bad decisions as a teen that cost me a lot of pain. There is nothing else for me to do now accept move forward. My pain is my pain living in all of me who am now reading about me.

71. Darkness wanted to consume me and send me away to her lower worlds, but I have come to my senses realizing while still alive and breathing on top of mother earth soils. I have a chance to be healed from these wounds and the wounds I have dished out at me. I'm not just conjuring up words to please me who am reading about me.

72. I'm not frightened any more by the world of dreams that showed me my destinations. Fear was always walking beside me and I didn't know. Ignorance is deadly and can wipe us into extinction. I know that's a heavy word but if we think about it for a moment we know reality when we read, hear, see, and feel the truth.

73. This world is being dictated by lower emotions who is intercepting man's emotions resting on the left hand side, left hand side, where?

74. We'll talk more about us later. I'm speechless now from emotional beside me. Weakness has stirred from motion pictures playing within. Apart of me is just emotional about now. I'm crying deeply,

soul deeply, soul deeply, Soul deeply, soul deeply. I can't even speak clearly right now. Weakness has gotten the best of me for a moment. Please bear with me. I've never Felt and have understood in my younger days a love for me that is so authentic. I can positively and humbly say that I love all of me who am reading these words. Even I alone haven't read these words. I Just want to let me know I love me that is also in you all living with no homes and no food, struggling to feed your families, soul deeply cries, soul deeply cries, soul deeply cries, Soul deeply cries, soul deeply cries, soul deeply cries! Mother help us men find you who am reading about me this very moment. I recognize without you we are not men only slaves to cold hearts and calculations. In my house I don't want that to be the end of this story. Joy is good but without gentleness walking beside me I'm just a productive problem waiting to erupt into the earth's stratosphere like yellow Stone Park with no warning. All it takes is one thought of sensual scenes mentally to trigger lower emotions, but that does not mean I have to give in.

74. Good Cheer is on my side. I know nothing can tear me down unless fear rules, but this day my power house is forever and more.

75. I'm really glad to be able to walk in order with the law of spiritual me living, controlling this natural physique. I'm a say it again I can become my own worst problem and enemy without even knowing. The outside looks on seeing, but we can't even see ourselves.

76. The world of fear wants to send me away; not me I'm a walk with me until these wheels fall off. Honestly I can say the joy I possess relieves the stress. Mother dearest sits while I'm remaining still directing and producing; truly this is a word to me.

77. I can stand in peace knowing my soul is unmovable and still walking by my side.

78. The one seated beside me on the left hand side beneath the crane holds fear; I want me that am in you readers to know that it only takes one wrong move through this tongue and mouth and body language to set her off. Title waves and tsunamis is her—emotions, and if I'm not prepared or in my place as man. I'm like Samson becoming a victim to myself; surely I'll be chewed up like salami on light bread makes me think of a subway, foot long. That's just me personally.

79. There is an awful emotion that intends to bury me quickly into mother earth's soils, but this day I'm a live with me and express all of me to you who are reading these words of wisdom.

80. Right about now I'm feeling pretty good. Hey! Nothing can replace the truth for real. I'm just happy to be walking and being with people on earth just like me. I know we are willing to change deep down, soul is distracted by materials, where are the hero's! Where is neo for crying out loud! Deep down I know it's going to be OK. Did you readers feel that emotion reach away from self, the key is to know me. This is the only way the soul can overcome the generational curse pass down through millenniums and centuries, real talk from I, the dominate one in speech resting materially, left hand side is where Jesus Christ tapped into me verbalizing words of encouragement, enlightenment, hope, salvation to all of me. The one resting on the right hand side tempted me, earthly and sensual is the one who has claimed more souls all because of one thought and there goes the neighborhood. No really! There goes the neighborhood.

80. Apart of me wants to be master and lord over me with just one thought as I have explained over, and over again to me. This is a movie internally

manifesting for real genuine, and can become a nightmarish place or a paradise, I'm not a victim no not this time around. Personally I'm walking confidence turning every little doubt into creativity. Not I, but my helper who walks with me daily. Can we all say at one time and as one mind amen on three? One, two, three, Amen!

81. Soul is so prophetic myself is spreading cheerful vibrations, but we all know man is dead weight without rhythm and soul language, who is in all of me, who is reading this very moment.

82. I, the dominate one, Yes I am the one controlling speech, and yes I am the man spirit who walks among my peers, haven't you read about me I'm in all who are hungry enough and determined enough to stand for good and right. Surely I can smile expressing good cheer, so I speak to all of me out side to be in good spirit for I am my helper and protector when I am recognized.

83. You who are reading about me know that at times we really didn't have it all together and still we don't, but I have protected me when we truly prayed and meditated. Again I, alone cannot win only we can win; together we harmonize bringing us to a spiritual communion not of material things. My communion is inward. I love me, now here is

a rhyme for me out there. Along side of me there is sorrow and fear. No escaping just recognized she's there. Surely I can stand and walk with beautiful soul that is a part of me forever and more. God Is surely present so nothing can have me only her, but this time the apple isn't mine. Together where spreading electricity in the mind. God Is present so this is not a moment to tremble, don't walk in defeat Jesus Christ walks on water so can I; this frame is physical but let's get a spiritual work out, let's get sound, what a wonderful word of life it's now in me. Peace is real genuine unmovable again I said it, by my side where dynamic duos like batman and robin, still going, still on both feet on planet rhyme. We continue on to the afterlife, we continue on living life peacefully with no erroneous or evil seeds suppressing this place of sobriety. The real reality is what we call it, isn't creativity a beautiful art made by God? Honesty has a place with God, and just remember I am the dominate one in speech, and everybody reading say it with me, Amen!

84. Let me just say I am not intending to spook me out with these upcoming words. These words are to bring insight from emotional that walks with us all. The word sounds, reads, and has the characteristics of a man. So for you readers stay

aware and alert or else you can fall away from me that am in you.

85. I am the left sphere who keeps the truth written; I only verbalize things and write out problems on paper. I am not poetry and a movie theater, but we must work together to bring peace on this earth. I am not the poet and singer. I'm good cheerful emotions my spirit is man manifesting through the whole frame, without me there is no head or leader ship in place, there is no peace, real peace. I play a major role as well as my neighbor resting beside me wearing soul and effeminate language; God is present.

86. The word lowly made a part of me think in pictures while I'm changing this message into words. Straight out of the tongue it goes where it fall only my soul that is a part of me will know and recall a past event. If I'm not connected or in harmony with my soul there is no smiles on this face in the mirror or even me reading about me this very moment. Truly it doesn't matter where I go there's no running and hiding from me forever, fear is a persona holding one's own fate, but the key is to stay in our place by recognizing our own house. She—emotions is a magic potion promoting effeminate motion coast to coast dwelling in all of me, yup! In you too who is reading about me

that is also in you. Everybody reading with me say, amen!

87. Here are some more words from me. Joy I possess relieves the stress—by the way when you read this verse you can see I am being influenced by poetical my neighbor working beside me. I can see through the right eye, the whole world looks brand new to me truly I know what it means to be born again emotionally running at the same time in spirit. I don't play games with my soul anymore. I see too many saints letting go of the harp while I was still in prison predicting praying and meditating a dream one day will come true. There I go with me spewing out words just call them a global (killer) healer. Words so deep I'm bringing up secret underground bunks, now I'm in awe looking thinking fire is for real sitting stored up in my belly. The whole world as I speak is under insanity; this very moment I can be free as well walking in love wearing perfect health, even though every side walk looks panicky, flesh, muscles, and bone in the face is turning plastic, I'm a just call it as I see it, mannequins. I love me because I was once a face of disorder and sending mixed signals, but at the end of the day, this new day of hope awaits me all that am reading about me. I love me that am in you, stay encouraged; truly this is a word to me.

88. I'm not defeated this time around. I can stand with me every moment of the day; I don't play around with soul. The whole world is a great stage, the crowd responds to my emotions. Where now swaying side to side knowing this body is made of earth's soils, Wow! So no matter what we do in this earthly life I can either hate or love thee; truly this is a word to me.

89. When we mix cold reason with hate you have a callous malicious joyous face. That isn't too good, not at all.

90. If I don't know me every facial and body language is like a puppet being pulled by unseen strings, playing using, leading the whole frame downstream. That isn't good at all; truly this is a word to me.

I AM MY HELPER TO ME (PART 1)

BOOK ONE, CHAPTER TWO

Today you and I must take responsibility for gestures and body language. Chris levitates like Jesus movements. I'm rooted in genuine humility wherever I go I'm spreading real genuine liberty with my right hand in the air like lady liberty. Free at last makes me think of Dr. King.

2. I am unique in every way, accepting all of me seated beside, truly, I am peculiar releasing from the tongue and mouth words of awe sending electricity from city to city, town to town; I am my helper to me.

3.   I have to get this off my mind; I have been such an effeminate mess remembering me around seven and my eleven year old cousin, we discovering one another. Mom and his mom was in a shock, do I remember what she spoke to me about? I can't remember. Mom showed mercy and loved me, she kept an eye on me personally I was going through all types of emotions, for real. Internally I was fighting and losing this internal battle, shyness was who I became to be, for years and years. When it came to down to sports like basketball, which was my ticket and outlet to expressing all of me to the eyes watching my abilities. As of today I am confident enough to walk with me accepting my weakness. Though the struggle continues I know that I am not alone. There am always another me out there who am struggling to hold on to the wisdom. She is all up in the scripts, 'Get wisdom and insight! Do not forget or ignore what I say. Do not <u>abandon</u> wisdom, and <u>she</u> will protect you; love <u>her</u>, and <u>she</u> will keep you <u>safe.</u> Getting wisdom is the most important thing you can do. Whatever else you get, get <u>insight.</u> Love wisdom, and she will make you great. Embrace her, and she will bring you honor. She will be your crowning glory.'" proverbs 4:5-9 NIV. I am my helper to me. I can testify to the fact, I'm still here, soil and spirit walking on soil. Truly I have been blessed knowing my world would've ended

years ago, opportunities and second chances just don't happen, mercy was avail. I also prayed for myself and for the ones who are also given second chances.

4. Apart of me isn't happy at all. This is an everyday battle. In the wilderness while devilish sphere intends to wear me down. I'm going to always recognize. Emotional is on the control boards commanding the left hand, foot to move on the world stage, don't know me my brothers and sisters reading about me that is in you It's like walking straight in front of a one hundred mile per hour Lamborghini, this isn't funny, and I love all of my precious souls and will never lead me astray from real inner peace, for real genuine, one hundred percent. Truth is, as long as I'm in communion realizing breaking words into rhythmic motion. We will flow across the borders state lines arising on arising, state to state awakening feeble minds walking the streets hungry for soul, knowledge, and understanding. There coming from gutters from all over uttering rhythmic potions releasing innocents to the populations abroad. Lyrical little Gods I call them, don't never forsake me! Title waves arise from inner world commotions; I am my helper to me.

5. It's midnight, Imaginations pull and tug, emotions are playing major roles, soul is willing. I'm a keep on keeping on. My self-interest is in peace and recognizing my place. Staying true and honest, my man Jesus Christ is the only one triggering her-emotions. Soul is doing just fine, thank you for asking; I am my helper to me.

6. The truth is it's been a battle to the point in this life that there needs to be a little sharpening and changes to my character. I have told untrue stories that made me feel bad at the same moment. My heart just can't take telling stories. Sooner or later I will spill out from the tongue. There are some things that should not be told, truth brings trouble on to the stage if love is not the base.

7. It's a sad sight to see us being yanked, pulled around it's like one moment joy shows up at the same time fear is lord over, dictating every move. I know me that am in you who is reading, that you can learn to grasp and understand my words of wisdom. It's going to require growing pains which we all know we must face in this body made of dirt and soil. This is real emotions dwelling in us all from coast to coast. Wherever I am there is a department called mixed emotions running up and down the streets. Today I choose to be a problem solver using words, actions filled with

fire that quickly inspires, attracts, I'm the right hand man. Let the presence of God be known. In the past I didn't know my left hand from my right hand emotions, for real genuine. I didn't know the difference so fear was lord over everything I did. Fear and earthly me ran together. I was afraid of me; on top of that there were confused emotions. Personally I said to myself, 'I don't want to be living the rest of my days miserable, sick in the mind, body at twenty and climbing. That moment tears were flowing and me I was crying like a little baby wanting mommy. Later on I believe it was March 8, 2000 I decided to grab hold of the words of wisdom. The bible. I was at the end of days—I mean I couldn't keep lying to myself. emotionally disturbed since elementary so hyper, a fire cracker, dipping and dappling in things where I shouldn't be doing, extremely passionate, but I've come to find out that I didn't have the tools to direct my emotions, only thing that interest me was basketball and being held which lead to relations at twelve with a sixteen year old male. Females were like me but confusion disfigured me causing girls to want to mentor me and understand all of me. I had a clue but fear sent me back into hiding. Why I was getting smiles from girls? Some seen and felt my spirit vibe, at that time I had no clue why I was being watched. So I took it and ran with it whatever it was, personally my world inwardly was messed up, for real. If I knew then what I know now I wouldn't be, but today I am at peace and moving forward is the next chapter. To all of me reading about me that is also in you be a blessing. Turn dark energies into a light of real peace; recognize the devilish spirit who possesses lower vibrations and is never on vacation, for real; truly this is a word to me. Living and growing up in the housing authority or as we say the projects on 220 Custer St in Stamford, Connecticut was personally for me an experience. Now that I look back I have truly learned from my errors. At a young age I've learned to never join a crowd because if one does wrong you might just get all the blame from the crowd. Don't ever play the role of a tough guy or a bully when there is always someone out there might look weak but you come to find out that you went over the borderline by talking like a big shot. I had some close friends I grew up with, L.J. was one we knew each other since we were like five years old. As kids we went to school together and like boys. We fight, but we were kids. As we grew older we kind of went our separate ways. Elementary began and I was beginning to feel at an early age strong emotions. Didn't know what emotions were at the time. I liked everybody it was love at the beginning stage and I mean I was for real. The problem is just I was so shy it was ridiculous. One thing for sure I was one of the fastest and one of the most athletic. I can say that now! I did have something and oh yeah! I imitated Bruce Lee, Michael Jackson, MC hammer, who didn't! old R & B and Karate back in the mid-eighties that was one of my charms I used effectively. I also wanted to race everybody I came in contact with; one to race, one to race, one to race, but there was one I just call him D. He was fast and furious I knew there was going to be a time we were going to race. Then it finally happened in the spring near end of the school year. The school always have Field day. I was waiting for one event. The fifty yard dash. Then it happened we met up and it was like the match of the decade. He beat me by a tenth of a second. I believe that was my most memorable moments during my young days. Middle school it was now 1992. I was in the sixth grade a time when music really was a part of my life. This was the year I began writing stories, poetry and lyrics from all types of music. I remember how I used to copy the lyrics and memorize it and let it out in school. I knew there was something there in me, but I didn't know what it was honestly. Around this time we were struggling to the point we needed to make ends meet. My oldest sister K.K. at the time was working but we needed extra so the little bit we did have we began to sell oatmeal pies, sub sandwiches,

Pickles, Soda's and Juices. I've learned through these hard times that no matter how hard it gets there is hope; I believe this was my first job right here at home. and an experience showing me that I can survive and didn't have to sell drugs even though I've seen kids my age and a little older than I on the corner clapping (Exchanging). I personally never got involved but felt tempted one time when I see someone I knew with a roll (big dollar bills). Instead I didn't do it. I had my own problems and these problems were emotional turmoil, a tug of war between I must admit and be honest, so if you want to condemn me that is fine because this is personal me I am sharing with you from the soul. I was struggling with this emotional effeminate persona and this strong and bold young man who could not understand what was happening within. One moment I have deep feelings; Then the next time I'm feeling this way. I needed some real understanding on how to deal with these emotions, and it seem like one moment I'm fine but the next minute I didn't know how to express myself like I wanted to because I felt like it was wrong to be this way, and so I closed up and remained in a shell. School just added to the insecurities. I was truly a problem and my nightmares was consuming and compassing me, who knew? Only me, that is in millions.

I was hungry for a better and deep down I still kept hope alive, but had no knowledge to face fear, only thing I knew was music, hand wash my clothes, sugar and bread in the refrigerator, roaches ganging up on me from the ceiling and on the floor. There coming from everywhere even if we did spray those roaches with some raid. We still needed a pest bomb I don't know what kind, but we needed one for real. It was also the time I was consumed in video games, basketball, hormones, and trouble in the neighborhood. If there were a rehab center for video game addicts. I was overdosing and near death literally. I ate and slept video games, from dusk till dawn, for real! I used to tell mom I'll be at my friend A.B. house for an hour come to find out I would be there for hours playing video games. Coming back home at night knowing I was in trouble; I knew then that there were no more video game playing for a good while. One time A.B. and I were really becoming video game junkies to the point we lived in the bowlarama / arcade. I was starting to pick up some bad habits and I mean our addiction as young kids around eleven and twelve had lead me to steal from mama pocket book forty dollars. I didn't tell A.B. about it but he was clueless any way. He was just ready to go to the arcade. So we went to the bowlarama loaded exchanging fives and tens for rolls of quarters. We played rampage and double dragon until we beat the game. But when it was all over we knew we had to face reality. The reality that the wrath of mama was nigh. I knew she was worried and looking for me. It was the walk home that had me praying that I go to heaven now! I mean just rapture me out of here on a one way ticket! Knowing the end of days was near. I took deep breaths, inhaled and exhaled as if I'm about to dive into some cold ten foot swimming pool hoping I don't drown. God had to be with me because when I walked in the door. I had already known my arms, legs, and butt was coming off. When it was all said and done not a thought nor did I ever attempt to steal from mama or anyone ever again. God had to intervene on my behalf through grandma prayers because I still had my arms, legs, and butt still attached to my sinews and bones. I didn't know anything about the bible at that time, but I knew then a prayer was real man! Grandma had to be praying because I thought judgment day was coming quick. After this horrific movie was over I slept like I was three again. Because of my addiction of playing video games and so much back and forth trading, we were like the internet; get connected. I traded until one day it all came to a head. When games begin to start disappearing, everybody was like where's my game! Where's my game man! It wasn't just me but most of the kids in the neighborhood were sneaky and video game addicts. I wasn't the only one trading off games and the only video game addict, but anyway this was a neighborhood crisis. Well, more—I mean more than a handful wanted to pin it on someone, so guess who got the pin? Yes! Your right this time, ME! I believe it was about eleven of them confronted me; I must admit that I had some lost video games as well but this was just strictly hate. I was across the street from home. All housing is the same design and I was being surrounded in the parking lot near the cars. I said to myself,' I'm not about to get my butt beat down! I knew if I can make it across the parking lot I'm near the house, so I ran down the steps, I was running for my life, I was fast I knew none of them couldn't catch me, but as I looked straight ahead of me there was another one of those bullies just happened to be standing there talking to someone until he seen me running, I knew in my mind he was helping them boys out. He reacted I reacted, even though he was little bigger then I was I put a move on him but he caught me and through me down while the eleven other boys were running my way. As I was thrown to the grass one behind me stomp me in my back, I—mean it wasn't one of those stomps like your dusting off one of your shoes, this was like one them knee above head stomps. That's the best way I can put it, but thank goodness one of my sister friends slash associates came in and stopped it all or else I would've really been hurt bad or even worse. It was she that came to my rescue. Thank God for making me a suitable helper. Amen. As I got older eighteen years old and barely graduating from high school only by the help of one teacher who truly wanted to see me graduate. After school was out I moved down south to Opp, Alabama because I had nowhere else to go. I didn't have No driver's license all I had was a few things and headed south. It was my eighteenth birthday when I decided to enroll into the technical college in opp, Alabama in 1998. To make a long story short I spent two years welding and taking classes and didn't finish. Inner conflict and anger was my problem, I was my problem and knew it. My anger raged in me I didn't know how to release this rage, only thing I did when I went home was get my pellet gun and shoot cans and bottles, I even shot at a dictionary, after that it was taken away from me, which I thing was the best thing to happen because I was getting more warped and becoming more of a problem to myself. One year has passed and now twenty and determined to do better. I had only one book at the time and that was a bible. I read and read and read, carried the bible to work on the job in my back pocket, which was after I had already quite school to go to work at Clark trailers in Andalusia, Alabama for a while but I wasn't making enough money. so I decided to go to work in opp at Johnston Industries March8, 2000. I was still walking hard, my ways were too hyper active; good worker and willing to learn the job though. At the age of twenty two my worst nightmare has now been revealed, fear has now swallowed me up into the land of oblivion, One hundred percent genuine. My life was at stake, didn't know what was going on, I was still on my job working until I heard all the commotion. Now here I am one day in the county, a bonds men came to my aid, all I wanted to do was get out so he set up a payment plan, four thousand gone just like that. Sitting in the town and state of Opp, Alabama for three years, couldn't leave the state. So **personally** I was already in prison. Everything I have ever wanted to do that was good was slipping away every breath I've taken. What a horrible time as I watched mom and grandma sit with me. I can never forget it was august 22, 2005 four days after my 25th birthday, slowly watching as I was being taken away by authorities. For the first time in my life I was going to be removed from the outside world, rock me to the marrow all the way to the soul. Real talk my brothers and sisters. Two months in the county then send away to the big house to be processed, given numbers, finger printed, shaved heads, new clothes, slipper sneakers you know, sort a like ked's. If we didn't do what we was told or even make up our beds we would get either put in lock up or even get the club. I spent my two months there before I was transferred to a medium custody prison. While waiting for the train—I mean the transfer bus came and I was doing all what I supposed to do, even though this prison was a max five I was doing my two months with paper and pen, rhymes, poetry, reading my bible and even reading other religious literature, but I had moments fear was intending to take me out. I wasn't about to go under this way, fear is powerful but I was going to do whatever it was to find stability in a place where there is nowhere to go and hide. Thank God for giving me and creating in me joy and creativity. I used her-emotions that are a part of me to write real genuine poetry, straight soul the piece of me that was boiling over ready to erupt to the surface who has kept hid and in the darkness for decades. No more will she be hidden from the light. Late that December I was transferred to a medium security prison. I am now twenty five years old in a place with souls that will never get out of prison. There are some who look at this place as home; get a wife and live happily ever after, for real. Knowing the truth about me triggered her—emotions. I did not let her that lives in me to stray away, I kept my promise to me to not to sell my soul to the sickest of minds in a place where there is only chow call, gym call, yard call, church call, and pill call. Then it's back in the hole with forty plus guys in one block cell with urges to get at me or someone else. I am glad that I did not sell my soul. As a man I have kept her that is a part of me from disrespecting herself in front of me. I have witnessed during my four years and some change that there are rules that you have to recognize if you don't want to get hurt in this place. Number one do not mess with a man's wife in prison, number two do not join the crowd, you are putting yourself in harm's path way. Number three don't let anyone disrespect you, and don't disrespect others. do not let no one get over by bullying you or threatened your wellbeing or else that soul will think of doing it again and the next time can bring drama and even more prison time on your record. Stand your ground with always a word of wisdom and knowledge rooted in love in all that you do. The scripts say, 'For our struggle is not against flesh and blood, but against rulers, against the authorities, against the powers in this dark world and against the spiritual forces of evil (ignorance) in the heavenly realms.' Therefore put on the full armor of God, so that when the day of evil comes, you may be able to stand your ground, and after you have done everything to stand. Stand firm then, with the belt of truth buckled around your waist, with the breast plate of righteousness in place, and with your feet fitted with the readiness that comes from the gospel of peace. In addition to all this, take up the shield of faith, which you can extinguish all the flaming arrows of the evil (ignorant) one. Take the helmet of salvation and the sword of the spirit, Ephesians 6:12-17. NIV. Which is the word of God.'" the word extinguish means to put out (fire) or put an end to; quench. And to overcome fear is to recognize, understand, distinguish, and control. As time passed I began to get wiser, stayed busy writing, figuring and solving problems, growth inwardly help me become a force. The weapons I was carrying were installed and no one could stand in thy presence, truly this is a word to me. Along this journey I've seen drama and uncontrollable emotions, fights, busted heads, one against five, brawls, fighting amongst themselves over television, sports, and gambling. Through it all I must admit to me that my emotions didn't get the best of me I let myself get into a friendship with a man named H. M. my first two years, I told my grandmother about him and she seen him on the visiting yard. He was ten plus years older than I was. I was twenty five years old. He had a life sentence and was not getting out any time soon. He told me about how this system ran and about the history the first time I met him. Soon he would have to transfer to another camp, reason was not fully explained. In two thousand eight this guy named M. J. that I also told my grandmother. He was a short guy but was also a man who had much time. He wanted the best for me and wanted to see me do well out there when it was my time to depart from prison. He was a lot older then I was about ten plus years then me. He intended to give me his number; I knew this was the end. I came to my end and soon I was on my way out of prison. I learned that prison is what you make of it. You can face reality before you and take advantage of the opportunities of the education and books that is offered to you. Prison can be either a college or a real prison house for you mentally and spiritually. Take this word from me, I know. Learn all that is available to you. So when you enter the real world you can have hope knowing that I am not my worst enemy this time around. Amen. I have learned that my fears were facing me, this day nothing can separate me from love, boldly I can come to the throne because I am somebody and nothing and I mean nothing can defeat me. I understand and can distinguish my weakness from my strength.

February 3, 2010 was my day and I didn't want to ruin my chance. My good time over some foolishness because if I did I would do the whole ten year sentence which means I wouldn't be getting out until 2015. That isn't a good feeling.

I tell you though when I had a place to stay my heart was relieved honestly. When the officer said, King! Pack your stuff! It was like—first I did feel a little excited, but I was confident knowing I have faced my biggest enemy, me. And I was shown respect because I carried myself respectfully. I also learned that it could've not ended this way, it could've ended with me either in the hospital, shipped to a max prison level five, and with another charge added to the one I already have, but instead I wanted to get better not worse, it's easy to fall and get into some mess when you surrounded and nowhere to go accept on your bunk. Prison is not for little boys who think there bad and tough, trust me. I have seen these young fellows locked up and while in prison, this place in prison is called lock up and no I'm not talking about what you see on Tell-a-vision, I've seen what lock up is, it is not where you want to go for long periods of time. There was a man while I was in prison who committed suicide. I was ready to leave hell with my blue khaki's on and my light blue shirt on I was ready to go home. I am blessed to be one of the few to come out of the pit; truly this is a word to me. Today I'm spreading liberty to the left and right minds whose eyes cross over misguiding the left foot and right shoulder; truly I am my helper to me. I will always walk in faith no matter the weather. I know I coming out of the storms born again matured emotionally now the enemy surely can't have me; love is real together where making history.

8. Mildness this very moment gets the best of me whenever photo's play in me like a movie; truly I am my helper to me.

9. Who am I? I am the cheerful one beneath the crane of all, just remember without me there is no cheerful expression on the faces of the black men, red men, Hispanic men, china men, and the light skin men, real talk is mine from state to state, nation to nation I am, walking beside me together in unity then shall the kingdom manifest bringing real peace to the dis-tress; truly this is a word and I am my helper to me. This is the end of chapter one and two of my journal, the book of me with insights.

FEAR
(ANCIENT EMOTIONS)

BOOK ONE, CHAPTER THREE

Lefty says: "Those who are reading about me began to fear. I want me that am in you to know that whatever you do fear is there and can either be understood or denied. Fear is settled beside me on my left hand side. Fear can become my enemy or my helper. Fear isn't playing. One false move is all it takes for my speech to drown under the waves of emotional me.

Right says: Just know making money and loving all isn't a bad at all, fear though I'm possessing in my house better be recognized, my ways are emotional, Ms. Beautiful rhythmic, fear lives in all of me, and it doesn't matter what color your skin, you have an impulse your mine just in different flavors."

2. Lefty says: "Fear has dominated me for centuries, decades, millenniums, since the beginning. Fear has intercepted man's mind and he still today is intending to figure me out. Today man has a chance to find. I am the dominant one in speech; my emotions are positive sending good vibrations to billions of me from old country towns to the brightest city lights in America and around the world. I am not fear, fear walks beside me, and will not overcome my house.

    Right says: Motion pictures belong in me, and know I'm not happy, my house possesses creativity, music, poetry, and rhythm and blues. The world feels my emotions from coast to coast. Joy just plays a major role in moments in all."

3. Right says: "I'm alive whether I'm accepted or not; without me there is no art and music, for real. I'm a visual, musical poetic, just know also I'm a dreamer haven't you readers read about me, I'm all up in the scripts. Joseph was a dreamer tapping in to my ways, I'm the one interfering spreading melodies, and I'm the one sending enlightenment. Insight is mine touching communities. This is me working alongside of joyous holding speech. We do this only for me touching the world living and breathing outside in a world suffocating from a lack of knowledge. Moments of insight

spreads germ free, my name is love or call me Ms. Affection, swaying the hips to the sound waves of music. My music can bring harm, healing, or even world peace. Read the scripts some time, I'm all over, for real; personally I'm seeing me daily through life expressing my spirit to the world. I'm the controller, the motor and the motion. My ways are meekness, gentleness, without my emotions there is no sway a longs. My poetry is real resting in me forever and more, my home."

4. Lefty says: "Fear has misled generations away from knowing there true state of mind. I must counter then recognize my help. Fearful images and fearful emotions had my limbs that I'm controlling truly all out of whack. I mean fear in the past had me walking blind folded, for real. Fear has used these limbs and facial expressions to lower energy. This very moment fear wants all that I stand on. I'm letting all of me out there who am reading these words know without I, the land is filled with fear and sinister spirits with no law and order. Spirit energies possessing negative vibes are soon to appear. What this all mean? The devilish sphere is fear overcoming minds of men. Using me, and setting me up for great disappointment. I just want all of me to know joy is mine whether we walking on top of mother soils or not, joy is mine."

5. Lefty says: "You readers must know that without me there is no joy, no planning, and no order. There are only savages and animals upon the land, now filled with fear, death, depression, and violence. As I speak to the world outside this moment, billions have already been overwhelmed by awful emotions a long with movie pictures of horror. Am I intending to scare me not a chance I am just a messenger. My ways are positive and hopeful.

    Right says: I'm one who has rooted up foundations from its place, intelligence has turned backward, and this is how joy and education became my trophy. Fear is in my possession and now facials are sour expressing words of lowliness. There in touch with my emotions, question is my place rooted and unshakeable? If I'm out of order it's going to take me to get me in order with the help of real speech and actions.

6. Right says: My Fear has affected men in high places; some have tapped into my lower place, my energy.

7. Lefty says: "This cerebral knew this spirit man knew that lower emotions were intending to be lord and master over all that was good within. Today the awful emotions are speaking through billions of

me. Taking advantage over positive spirit energies; this is only temporal when storms of fear, anger and rage begins to overwhelm me. So many in the millions ended my existence physically, spiritually for those who end me wander, fear is now lord. For those who remain bold, courageous, humble and recognize. I am passing over to the other side in confidence and boldness, for real and I am genuine. Did you readers know when this earthly body trembles from the emotions of fear at the same time with pictorial images of horror. Those emotions better be known to self or else I'm out of order. How? There is no harmony and oneness, I, alone cannot win the battle without a suitable helper. Fear has dictated history through actions, head, face, arms, and legs, moving downhill on a road not clear. The only thing compassing is fear; you're now in the horrific movie scenes. Fear has been a part of man since created from her-man. I can run, hide, or face me. If I choose to remain in ignorance I'll be just like the men in the scripts, 'the might men of Babylon have for born (refused) to fight, they have remained in there (fear) holds: their might hath failed; they have become as women.' Jeremiah 51:30 KJV. This emotion of fear has been dominating behind the scenes of men, who thought there kingdoms would never fall. Fear has been acted out through violence, men of ancient of days were blinded and not realizing there murderous ways were based on a lack of knowledge of one's own existence. Fear shows up everywhere and then goes back into place after the wrath has been surfaced. The scripts say, 'Nineveh is destroyed, deserted, and desolate! <u>Hearts melt with fear; knees tremble, strength is gone; faces grow pale</u>.'" Nahum 2:10 GNT.

8. Lefty says: "Fear is in a world of one's own. Billions follow even though a few escaped her loose or the X worlds, billions are falling prey as we speak to the lower and distorted spirit energies."

9. Right says: "My fear is forever and more, souls, so while you readers reading about yourself. Get to know, train, and reprogram the mind's eye or else the head, mouth, facial muscles, and limbs truly will be out of order, for real and genuine. This is my insight straight from me. The scriptures reveal my ways saying, 'My flesh trembleth for fear of thee; and I am afraid of thy judgments.' Psalms 119:120 KJV. This isn't all of my doing, my fear doesn't overwhelm unless I'm giving permission by decisions and choices made; the spirit man walks besides keeping this whole frame sound and in my place, is personal, few are recognizing that without knowing how to control and putting fear in place. Fear is enslaving, Fear is out all over the place deceiving and being deceived by her own

ways. This is taking place from sun up to sun down.

Lefty says: Fear has taking billions and billions of us in our physical state back to the soils, for real and genuine I must say all this because of lack of knowledge of her emotions. In the mind where she is seated even today men fall victim to himself not realizing he has become his own worst enemy. Fear overcoming goodness shuts down my light, but at the end I am the head, the kick stand, and the good cheer Jesus Christ mentioned. My joy is everlasting; if you want to know me read about me.

Right says: Going back and seeing this confused and displacement from man in psalms 119:120 in the King James Version shows what can happen when my fear and man's mind are not in their rightful place, the result leads to chaos and great disorder. All it takes is one word, I'm just the opposite, holding in my possession is pictorials, movies, music, I'm automatic with no reason, survivalist is what I'm doing daily for me, pictures role triggering fearful emotions all around the world from coast to coast am to coast to coast pm, I'm forever and more, real genuine spreading deep insight to the hungry. I play horrific movies in all of me from nation to nation causing lips and knees to tremble. My emotion is lower energies. Haven't you read, 'I hear all this, and I tremble; my lips quiver with fear. Habakkuk 3:16 GNT. My fear is playing with you readers; I'm always finding ways to trigger my emotion. It may be through seeing and reading from the words just like you have read in Habakkuk or it may be through other literature, such as the Qur'an, the Catholic, Buddha and the list goes on. Music resting in my possession makes the world awakened to this inner life. Where controllers just take a look at the left hand, see it it's only flesh, I'm just the operator, motivator, administer spreading emotions seeing my spiritual language plus my energy ignite billions of me."

10. Lefty says: 'Your emotions have made my speech slurred. Weakness has brought my joy down to lowliness, but I will recover from this temporary drought I'm facing, for real, events have played in my life heavily. for others it has almost lead them to their end, read the scriptures, but in the mist of lower energies of fear, anger and depression comes reason, strength, hope, and faith. Scriptures read,' Sarah's Troubles.

It happened that Sarah, the daughter of a man named Raquel, was insulted by one of her father's servant women. Sarah had been married seven times, but the evil demon killed each husband before the marriage could be consummated. Look at you! You've already had seven husbands, but not one of them lived long enough to give you a son. Why should you take it out on us? Why didn't you go and join your dead husbands? I hope we never see a child of yours!" be for I continue in these scriptures you readers can see how emotional has taken over reason and has released into the air a strong dose of negative emotions, lower energies, and most importantly devilish spirit energies dismissing any positive or encouragement. her-emotions has taken over and consumed man's spirit of good cheer and reason, but as we continue Sarah is going to reveal my spirit of reason and hope to all of me that is reading these words of hope. Amen.

Lefty says: the emotions of hate are so powerful and deadly because fear is playing a major role. I've been where Sarah was, I have been overwhelmed by darkness. Malevolent spirit energies that intended to rule me. We'll talk later and now back to the scriptures. Sarah was so depressed that she burst into tears and went upstairs determined to hang herself. But when she thought it over, she said to herself, "No, I won't do it! People would insult my father and say, 'he had only one child, a daughter whom you loved dearly, but she hanged herself because she. Felt so miserable. 'Such grief would bring my gray haired father to his grave,

and <u>I would be responsible. I won't kill myself.</u>'"
TOBIT 3:7-10 GNT and Deuterocanonical/
Apocrypha.

11. Lefty says: "I have been beaten up and depressed
almost to the point of ending the road to life
that's in me. Like Sarah I was on the brink of
elimination. Reason stepped in with a thought
and had me thinking of the consequences, more
pain, more problems, unfulfilled dreams crossed
over in mind.

Right says: fear is active and alive in us all, no
matter where you readers and hearers go in life just
know my spirit is you, and think about walking
to the store, I'm there. Thinking about leaving
the country, I'm there. Thinking about going
camping, I'm there. Thinking about living in the
mountains far away from the rest of the world,
I'm there. So remember my antennas are what get
me that am in you from A to Z, real genuine one
hundred percent and no artificial additives, for
real.

Lefty says: 'I experienced fear on a level as a
young mind that made me believe even more, I
was already sensitive to energies, very sensitive at
some moments. After my grand pop passed away
in 1989; I was at the age of nine years old when he

passed. I've never seen my real father but any way back to my experience. Two years passed since the loss of my pops; I was always very intuitive—not me, but my helper living in me. One time—I mean I am speaking the honest truth when I say I have encountered something that put fear on both my head and shoulders, I experienced a very unforgettable sight that had me sweating down nearly drench in sweat because of fear. I cannot give you readers dates and times because I have no record, but I do know this is that it was late. It had to be around 12:00 and some change or 1:00 am in the morning. All I know I had to get up out the bed and go. In my house hold we usually cut off all the lights but on this particular night the stare case light was on. So any way as I was walking towards the opening of my door I say about a foot from it. I see a black smoking aura like a spinning tornado, you ever seen how a black tornado looks like when it touches down. I haven't seen one in real life with my eyes but this is how it looked. It was about five feet high and I can see right through it. No playing games, I mean I was terrified. I ran right through this, I was actually intending to run around it but instead I passed right through it. I didn't know what this was to tell you the truth, at that time my uncle Stacy (passed in 2003) was staying with us at the time. I ran next store into his room trying to wake him up, l look back outside and it was spinning slowly in my direction so I ran down the steps, truth is I didn't run down the steps. I jump down the steps like a frog, seriously. Ran towards my mother's room and started banging on the door. I opened the door and told my mother everything, well after a good thirty minutes to an hour I decided to go back up stairs and when I got to the top of the stairs it was gone. And have never seen it again in my life. I can only describe it as a miniature tornado. That's the best way I can describe this thing, for real." this happened in 1991.

12.   Right says: "I'm always singing, the tape recorders and camera's resembles what I'm doing twenty four seven and that is recording. I'm always taking in information from the senses recalling horrific movies, good happy moments, past experiences, billions still walk around blind folded not really truly understanding my foundation is real. Choosing fear is not an option, minus is what I'm seeing taking over minds of prosperity and sending the billionth me into worlds of fear. Fear is me souls better recognize. Cerebral is just another intelligent way of keeping us in touch with myself, just like you readers are named by names such as: Jonah, Howard, Denise, Joyce, Jeremiah, Daniel or whatever your name maybe. I'm not written language nor does my place hold spoken language.

My Earthly name is the right hemisphere. I'm the insight, the one who possesses fearful emotions from coast to coast; we do love coast to coast am show.'

13. Right says: "Flesh isn't me it's only my vehicle to express my language to billions just like me, yeah I'm everywhere but most importantly take a look in the mirror, isn't my spirit sizzling, I'm the one upturning left facial, muscles play it's role till my physical goes back to motherly rich soils, spirit is me. So that means what? Let me tell you readers, my spirit energies are forever and more; isn't my music touching worlds it's got to be in the billions within worlds, even the writer Jason has been influenced by me. Errors plagued him almost sending the whole frame straight to the grave along with them dreams seated beside him. He didn't stay defeated he's a miracle but if he slips away, he's know different from the ones defeated and in disorder and sickness."

14. Lefty says: "Millions just like me are recording horrific movies; I'm just the spokesman for me. My power station is filled with joyous emotions, but if I'm not harmonizing myself is walking paranoia. I told you readers that I am in all of you, so get to know my power house it is so peaceful and filled with peace once you find the

treasure. I am happy also that you have finally read about my joy that is in you as well. Where? I am living beneath that crown where surgeons opened up doing a little work, but that is only my physical, truth is you can only see my spirit and wind through body language. See me now? I will leave that answer for you readers to fill in. again I am just the spokesman for me that is also in you who is reading and listening to me. I cannot love without my helper. I am not even a complete man without gentleness who feeds me insight. I can verbalize to all of me who am watching through these eyes daily to all of us. These eyes are only camcorders. Her insight has been send to me so I can explain myself clearly while rhythmic motions help to express. Bringing unity, peace, and courage no matter how difficult the situation may seem all things are possible when there's unity. When there's unity God is present."

15. Lefty says: "Whether we accept ourselves or not we are the original cameras. Recording and taking pictures wherever we go. We fear our own existence. Fear has kept motion pictures alive, well, and active causing my speech to break down because of fearful images and emotions. Sound waves of terror are being recorded daily in billions who are walking as I speak this very moment into the traps of negativity, lower energies, or the scary

and creepy nights. This word and chapter was recorded on September 26, 2009.

Right says: My control is the left hand, man is my help, my time is now and forever reigning spewing music as well as fearful emotions from town to town, city to city, wherever my crown I'm either charming, inspiring or in fear. You readers love me; I'm you upturning the left brow, wow! I'm all over the world being deceived by me, influenced by me, afraid of me, running and even hiding from me, while the music still touches life's playing globally."

THIS IS A WORD TO ME (PART 2)

BOOK ONE, CHAPTER FOUR

Lefty says: "I can accept the measure of masculinity that is in me knowing I can walk with hope by my side.

>Right says: mass, mass, masculine. When you realize that without me your cold and calculating, I'll be back, terminator, you isn't whole just a walking totem pole, bible call you men walking stiff-necks, I'm saying it again.

2. Right says: "who is that nurturer, me. Minus with a gentle loving hand, must admit my hand is yours, just learn from me, man is my help regardless what I'm spewing from the mouth and tongue,

words of light may come, but at the end I'm still me wearing my lower feelings.

Right says: She has been talked about and admired throughout history. Men married <u>me</u>, written literature, poetry, songs, even dancing. She is this very moment looked upon with soul and grace, sending out into the atmosphere levels of tears of love through beautiful melodies."

3. Lefty says: "I see me in my condition this very moment; I am not letting negative conditions around me influence, dictate my facial and body language; truly this is a word to me.

Lefty says: I write every thought down on paper with the right hand I'm controlling every moment and using. I do this when feeling overwhelmed by awful emotion intending to take me under. Knowing my ways is a blessing, and yes I am a living witness being affected by pain and anguish. Disrupting my speech, that is mine. I have learned to have faith in who I am. Nothing can separate me becoming one, expressing the Real God of peace and not the god of this world who is sending out mixed spiritual energies; truly this is a word to me."

4. <u>Lefty says: "who is the god of this world you might ask? The god of this world is no different from all of you or me out there. The problem is when I say mixed emotions it is like putting oil into water knowing it is harmful. The god of this world wears skin and holds the same emotions as I do. Knowing me is the key to deeper insight and understanding; truly this is a word to me.</u>

<u>Lefty says: Without me there is no speech.</u>

<u>Lefty says: hate pulls and nags on me, but my home is secure, motivated and excited to live again.</u>

Case One

<u>Lefty says: one time I asked a man a question I said, 'can you imagine or think of eternity? This man says, 'I see light surrounded by darkness.' this is all he said to me and walked away. this was recorded on November 17, 2009</u>

Case Two

<u>Lefty says: there was another subject as I would say, I ask him or her the same question to see what he/she would say and how would he/she respond.</u>

I said,' can you imagine or think of eternity? This subject I would call them said, 'Eternity could mean eternal colors and everlasting life.' As I was hearing this I began to evaluate myself and let the pictures of flowers, light, rainbow colors, fruits all that popped into my mind. Right says: First of all pictures, imaginations and all that stuff is mine, you just speak it out loud, I'm video's and music to the ear, for real, now go ahead with your subject Mr. Man, reason, or whatever Mr. I'll be back, terminator.

Case Three

Lefty says: I asked the same question to another subject, 'Can you imagine or think of eternity? This subject says, 'According to the bible?' this is what all he said and nothing else and walked away.

Case Four

Lefty continues: I tested one subject to see and feel how he was going to respond. He was one of those guys who will trade, borrow, and sell store items for a bag of coffee or for some tickets to gamble on a football, basketball, and baseball games, but also this subject had education and studied religions as well; any way I began to walk toward this subject respectfully and ask him with a book in my hand saying,' Would you like to read my book that talks about emotions? This subject said,' I don't deal with feelings and emotions! I deal with facts.' He then walked away and sat back down in front of the television. I said to myself. 'When you're dealing with feelings your dealing with emotions.' This was on October 10, 2009."

5. Lefty says: the world outside can either fall, collapse or become renewed emotionally and spiritually. Lower energies continue to overcome my joyous ways, but I know I am not held in strongholds forever. I am the good cheer expressing my spirit on the faces of all of me wearing all types of skin colors; look in the mirror can you see me now. I can love me with the help of my helper seated beside me.

   Lefty says: I will not let doubt overcome my house."

6. Right says: "I'm music, though my fearful emotions in billions have been understood only by a few and misunderstood by billions; Soul is what I'm expressing, even leaders were overwhelmed not truly knowing my fear is master and lord over spirit man. Just look at me throughout his-story.

I'm affecting, disturbing, and defeating doctors, lawyers, singers, poets, preachers, actors, officers, dancers, soldiers, psychologist, teachers, yeah even mechanics, foreign leaders, American hero's, mom's, dad's, never seen dad, musicians, football, basketball, tennis, track field, acrobats, wrestlers of all types, baseball players, mayors, presidents from all over even foreign lands, white skin, light brown skin, brown black skin, or whatever skin you wearing that's just a coat. The real me is emotional energies, spirit is me, this list goes on.

Lefty says: Hate, anger, sensual, and fear pulls and nags at me, my place cannot be defeated as long as I am in place of safety.

Right says: I'm a say again if you readers don't know emotions surely I'm a have you walking in a trance, horrific images plays a scene striking up emotional, me. You see now how easy and fast it takes to overwhelm. Now if you reading these words and still blind folded. Fear that is me truly has made a throne as lord over every action and speech; truly this is a word to me."

7. Lefty says: "I can admit that fear is not my house. Fear must recognize one's own self to be in complete harmony with herself and I with her-emotions. There are billions like myself out there who are

triggered by lower energies, but cannot rightly divide nor can I that is in them distinguish who is who. There are thousands of me, there are millions of me, and there are billions of me, the question is how many will find my identity in its wholeness? May these words lead me back to the sacred world of peace; truly this is a word to me.

Right says: Insight is mine. Seeing the whole pictorials is for real, this is what I'm here to do; bringing insight is one way I'm sending out to my man lefty to verbalize from that slithering tongue words deeper then wishing wells, deeper then earth's mantle and hot as the core; hotter than core more money means more knowledge, now I'm expanding insight that I'm possessing to the whole world causing generations to grow strong. The self; coming back home to their senses remembering me with pictures. This is all resting in my house. Where? The world of science call me the right sphere, religions call me the spirit of lowliness; truly this is a word to me.

Lefty says: From the sense of hearing—or let me say from the ear gate. I have heard and witnessed many words verbalized from me out there. Who didn't realize there birthing new seeds of fear, creating monsters of terror. There nightmares have advanced and my help don't even recognize my soul that is in them is lost and blindfolded by my own fear. That is in all you who are reading these words this very moment. I am not intending to scare me back into hell; free me from me and become renewed and live forever in peace. I like—I mean I love beautiful mansions don't you? Yes sir.

Lefty says: so let's unwrap the wound and get the dirt completely out, it hurts, but if I am going to heal I must face and accept all of me; truly this is a word to me.

Lefty says: You Right. I'm a say this to you. You know you're easily influenced by words, images; you're overcome by your own self. I am joyous sending good vibes to hungry nations, but I am still going to need my help. Right says: You see how my ways influenced your speech? There are great meltdowns, yes there is, and I'm one who plays a giant role in the movie biggest scenes, so get to know me."

8.   Right says: "I'm causing pain, left half side, isn't it better to know me then to fall away for not knowing me? Keys are now avail so now what you going to do run and hide from my pain and fear? Here is your chance my brothers and sisters.

Lefty says: where recording words and images whether its terror and an experience of joy and happiness. Where recording everything we see through the lens. Television or let me say the one eyed box is showing our errors and our strengths daily. Question is are we learning?

Lefty says: listen, read and take notes for it is time to get understanding.

Lefty says: Today I have intended awaken me from the long rest of disorder and confusion that I have obeyed for decades. This word has been recorded on December 30, 2011. This is the end of chapters three and four.

I AM MY HELPER TO ME (PART 2)

BOOK ONE, CHAPTER FIVE

Right says: "I'm my helper to me every moment. Swaying hips to the left to the right. Graceful is my movements upon this earth. Truly I'm worth. Beauty is what I'm manifesting and surely there is no second guessing. My ways are not mechanical. Soul and rhythm is mine. I'm seeing my language is not being nurtured. You deny me causing minds to walk one sided sending out mixed energies. You chose to walk after confusion and disorder. Just know without me there is no inspiration in the land; truly I am my helper to me.

Right says: I'm triggering the hearts of all around the world with my emotions.

Right says: we know I'm emotions. I'm the one causing hearts to pound, cold sweat, flight and fright has the limbs trembling. It only takes one scary picture to cause tummy aches and butter flies. My emotions had Saul ready to take David out the picture for good. He didn't want David to prosper. My anger, hate and jealousy consumed David. The scripts say,' Saul was <u>angry</u>; this refrain galled him. "They have credited David with tens of thousands," he thought, "but me with only thousands. What more can he get but the kingdom?" and from that time on Saul kept a <u>jealous eye</u> on David. The next day an evil (negative) spirit from God (was attracted to the negative spirit in Saul) came forcefully (consuming, overwhelming and perverting the spirit of goodness in Saul) upon Saul. He was prophesying in his house, while David was playing the harp, as he usually did. Saul had a spear in his hand and he hurled it, saying to himself, I'll pin David to the wall." But David eluded him twice. Saul was afraid of David, because the lord was with David but had (been overcome by negative spirit energies. Saul was drowning in fear and didn't know what to do except think of ways to murdering David.) Left Saul. 1 Samuel 18:8—12. NIV.

Right says: Soul is what spews out of me.

Right says: I'm always paving the way. Truly If I'm not in order I'm defeated by fear that is me. I'm soul cool and creative I'm always going to walk beside me. I'm always keeping me real and genuine. I'm always being soul. You know when the spirit man has recognized himself. Then there will be unity, oneness, and harmony between men. He will be called now the soul man; truly I am my helper to me.

Right says: Just know without emotional me there is no flow, singing, and soul hoppers. The world will be cold, dead, unfeeling, callous, malicious, soulless, and with no rhythm and blues. Haven't you readers read the scripts,' their hearts are callous and unfeeling, but I delight in your law. Psalms119:70NIV.

2. Lefty says: I would also like to say to all of me out there that without my positive emotions, my spirit. There is no peace only animalistic characteristics and no discipline. Right says: Facing me is every moment. I'm the one releasing melodies into the air, I'm the poet, athlete, singer, dancer, visionary, and dreamer. The scripts say, 'Here comes that dreamer!' Genesis 37:19NIV.

3. Lefty says: I've had moments I felt less of a man. Effeminate characteristics overwhelmed me;

this mouth and tongue was nailed shut. It's like mother came and took over my speech. I felt womanish. I then realized this isn't my emotion. This character isn't mine if you want to know the truth. I am always man, but I also realized if I'm not in place this meek spirit will overcome me. Women now even look upon me and see themselves. The question is can meekness and I walk in agreement and am be not of shame? I can say today surely I can. God is truly present when we come together.

Right says: Every man see's my spirit. There is nowhere for me to go, so my only choice is to accept me. The womb-man is only the physical coat. The spiritual I and my self are only known through body language."

4.   Lefty says: "I became weak from her emotions and had a little bit of man hood left to keep me from going insane and in torment mentally as well as spiritually. Isn't being soft and gentle is the opposite of what I am? I am mechanical, holding reason is the key to solving problems, but I tell the truth when I say, intending to find man that is me was a difficult; I'm still not where I want to be but I'm still am working toward betterment. So much confusion; I am seeing man's spirit in woman. My words are honest and sincere.

Lefty says: "I tell you readers the truth. The ones who will find me can endure her painful emotions seated beside me. For those who don't find I, will harm themselves, but I tell all of me who is reading these words. That there is hope for all; I am in all. I've been down for decades, but I have overcome my lower mind. There will be sensual impulses; the beast (self) will arise to the surface. The scriptures reveals inner emotional and spiritual battles saying,' Be self-controlled and alert. 'Your enemy (self/lower energies) the devil prowls around like a roaring lion looking for someone to devour.'" 1 peter 5:8 NIV.

5. Lefty says: "This very moment as I speak emotional storms intend to consume and defeat me.

    Lefty says: my speech is trembling but I am not defeated, for real. I've said it once I'm a say it again. No man can face himself face to face if fear is lord and master over spirit man; man is spirit.

    Right says: Man, man, man. What are you planning on doing now man? Starting a million man march. Go ahead! Just know I'm your music in your ear, I'm your music industries sending out my rhythmic vibes, isn't my soul reaching relieving stress and cold steps behind? Yes thank you, my mind is humbled by my originality, Jesus mentions my characteristics, tapping into me recognizing and preaching to all of me. This spirit man spoke through the physical male, (outer man) the tongue and mouth were only physical tools being used to send my electricity to all, listeners were very much in awe. My emotions can make all of us weep. My soul is emotional just take a look at the scripts, 'when Jesus saw her weeping, and the Jews who had come along with her also weeping, he was deeply (emotional) moved in spirit and troubled. "Where have you laid him?" he asked. "Come and see, Lord," they replied. Jesus wept. Then the Jews said, see how he loved (Lazarus) him.' John 11:33-36 NIV. I'm no game to be playing with my soul is real and will always minister to billions. Even though so many refused to accept and recognize that my emotions can have you readers either spewing sorrow, weeping and easily defeated by panic, it's my emotional waves, if not taught can lead the whole frame and my soul into spiritual, physical slavery. I'm seeing through the eyes of all of you readers with my ways remaining in bondage or free; this is a choice. No one can decide for you, your either an enemy or you have recognized my emotions; truly, I am my helper to me."

6. Right says: "Let me school you readers and listeners for a moment. That pain, that fear, that

love, that anger, and them sad emotions, surely! This is me, it's been said through spirit man, fear not. Looks like to me you still walking away from my sphere, full of flavor but no ice, because I'm not cold, callous and unfeeling is a no, no. nada. Mixing my ways with the man you get a hateful intellectual beast with no (soul) heart.

Right says: Yes, I'm admitting my gentleness wavers when unstable, singers and poets are mine sending out true feelings aligning billions of me all over the world. Singing is just one of my abilities touching, igniting sleepers to awaken, like a magnitude 10.0, soul is intuitive; soul is magical; soul is a musician; Stevie wonder, Ray Charles couldn't see but could see and hear, using me affective-lee, turning dreams and sound waves of music to reality, affecting presidents and your majesties from the U.S. to the U.K. isn't music mine living in that head of yours?

Right says: It's time to wake up!

Right says: All you readers and listeners have to do is call; truly, I'm my helper to me.

Right says: Tell you the truth my emotional ways are all over the scripts from genesis to revelations. There is always more insight in the scripts.

Right says: Human nature is sensual, devilish; opposite of cheerful and positivity igniting smiles from the east coast to the west; from the mid-west to the south east. You see I'm all over the world influencing me in all of you this very moment reading about my ways and what's in my possession, I'm soul, sitting in your dome my sons, fathers, brothers, mothers, and daughters. When them limbs move you know now I'm playing major roles wherever I'm present, haven't you read the scripts,' the lord was pleased with Abel and his offering, but he rejected Cain and his offering. "Why are you angry? Why that scowl on your face? If you had done the right thing, you would be smiling; but because you have done (wrong) evil, sin (negative spirit energy) is crouching at your door. It wants to rule you, but you must overcome it."

Right says: Born into this world soul lowly, seeing my mental ways, persuading taking Jason on a ride, used to have both his eyes defeated, he didn't know what took over his mind, fear and anger meant it taking control while self-mutilation played a role. I'm not my enemy unless you choose to be or isn't ready to face mirror image, isn't she soul beautiful? You will never recognize minus persuasion, charming billions that are listening, for good or for the bad, truly its decision making time, time is now just like the scripts. You know you like to shake those hips to the sound waves of music? Under the sun we come into this physical then depart. Reasoning is man every day of the week; he is only spirit like me arousing emotions, be of good cheer Is his aim and only together can we harmonize sending new minds back to the astral planes. This is where I'm a live forever and more. This literature doesn't come from outer world to be specific it's not coming from books out of libraries, straight from my dome. I'm just releasing me through my right hand man directing speech, broken down into poetical form; truly written language is under the influence of my knowledge possessing all of you readers and hearers wearing the (cranium) crown, you know just take a look at the left hand. That's what I'm controlling so just look in the mirror for once you will notice the left brow. I'm also controlling and then some, forever and more. Amen. Soul what is flowing out of me straight diving into mannish who's now spewing his own residence from the tongue and mouth words inspiring. Soul is my witness even back in Cain's day he let his brother by reason, personally I'm just my helper to me whether good or bad, my ways were mixing and mingling with the hand of man's reason leading astray with cold hate with jealousy as leader promoting the most devilish plots and planning. This is nothing but an evil potion created by thought with emotions of hate and jealousy. Madness mixing with happy isn't a match. Now this is what you call real world pollution spiritually and physically. The scripts say,' then Cain said to his brother Abel, "Let's go out in the fields." when they were out in the fields." Cain turned on his brother and killed him.

Right says: Then man had to nerve to say when lord asked Cain, "where is your brother Abel?" he answered, "I don't know. Am I (keeper) supposed to take care of my brother?" Genesis 4:4-9 GNT.

Lefty says: I was reading the scriptures today and because of this insight by my side. I have discovered that the one who created us; when I say us—I mean me and my helper. I am realizing that he is just like me or let me say I am just like the Creator of all. The scriptures say, 'So God created human beings, making them to be like himself. He created them male and female. Gen1:27 GNT.

Lefty continues: There is so much insight I am receiving right about now, truly I alone cannot release truth without my helper insight seated beside me. Thank you, God of the entire universe. Here are some more scriptures to confirm that I am just like the creator and the creator is just like me.

Lefty says: If you readers read real carefully you can see that <u>the creator knew</u> he was going to be <u>persuaded</u> (her) by himself when he first created himself. The scriptures say, 'then the lord God made the man fall into a deep sleep, and while he was sleeping, he took out one of the man's ribs and closed up the flesh. He formed woman out of the rib and brought her to him.

Lefty says: In another scripture you will see how I am persuaded by her-emotions within himself. Scriptures says: 'The <u>woman saw</u> how <u>beautiful</u> the tree was and how good its fruit would be to eat, and she thought how wonderful it would be to become wise. So she took some of the fruit and ate it. Then she gave some to her (No reason avail) husband, and he also ate it. The man answered, "<u>The woman you put here with me gave me the fruit, and I ate it.</u>" Gen.3:6; 12 GNT.

Lefty says: 'The creator had a feeling when his creation tapped into the knowledge of self. That there struggle and battle between good and evil would begin. This new beginning we see according to the scriptures was fear. Fear overtook them because this emotion was unknown; the creator let them know that since there decision was to eat, gain insight, understanding, knowledge and to satisfy the flesh. He would have to let them take full responsibility for their actions and choices in life. The fearful emotions will now either defeat them or Adam and his mate will learn to gain control of their emotional state, but for now both of them must face the consequences of not understanding what was already in them and that was negative emotions. The God, the creator of all things saw his own self through his creation. Emotions of fear, anger, sorrow, hate, joy, and love. The maker was feeling sad and expressing repentance or grieves when he witnessed himself thinking and acting out evil or wrongful actions through the facial and limbs. Truly, the emotional one has kept me under her-emotional sphere influence throughout his-story. The scripture reveals how the maker repents and becomes lowly according to what he has witnessed from his (people) self. The scriptures say: 'when the lord saw how wicked everyone on earth was and how evil their thoughts were all the time, he was <u>sorry </u>that he made them and put them on the earth. Genesis 6:5 GNT. In another translation it says,' the lord saw how great man's wickedness on the earth had become, and that every inclination of the heart was only evil all the time. The lord was <u>grieved</u> that he had <u>made (himself) man</u> on the earth, and <u>his heart was filled with pain. I will wipe (myself)</u> <u>mankind. Whom I have created</u>, from the face of the earth—men and animals, and creatures that move along the ground. Genesis 6:5-7 NIV.

Right says: you see how my emotions intervenes the entire universe. Musicians remember me in heavenly places. Magicians are using my ways influencing billions of me. My spirit affected all, motion pictures were avail triggering sorrow, tomorrow is another beautiful song, my melodies are mine; I am my helper to me."

My Journal, The Book Of Me With Insights

THE PROPSYPHATREES

BOOK TWO, CHAPTER SIX

Lefty says: "A man will set himself spiritually on fire whether it is to do good or bad. This all happens while he's still breathing and walking on the soils on top of father and mother's earth.

2. Right says: Yeah, and the heart responds to everything I'm doing. Hearts pound when fearful me interrupts intellectuals, degrees or no degrees I'm never going to change my mind is poetic and always pulling your chains and comfort zones. Did you readers just feel my emotions?"

3. Lefty says: "It only takes one insane or horrific picture to stir up a new internal battle for no

reason at all. This is why I am always pulling myself out of turmoil all the time. The stress may knock on my door, but I can make sure my joy and happiness gets the final good laugh."

4. Right says: "A part of me is joyful emotion and spirit. I'm upturning my facial cheek muscles, musical is not my problem it's a choice. Do readers want to make us sway or fall away, worlds and decisions count on me that is in you reader's. I'm no mechanic my hands only soothes the mannish seated by my mind, this is meekness souls will always sing and pledge allegiance.

5. Lefty says: A lover of self is not the problem. The problem is when the lower, higher spirit energies are out of order. Joy and happiness is now sick sending mix vibes, the bible call this unholy. I call it heavenly worldly-minded reciting poems and psalms.

Scratching only the surface only enables me to see joy, hate submerged binding minds true identity. Just thinking about what is happening in this world triggers emotional me. I'm overcome by sorrow, it only takes a thought to break me down; remembering me who once was a victim to fear, anger, and hate."

6. Lefty says: "Ignorance of who I am can keep these eyes in blindfolds.

7. Lefty says: Denominations are just that—divided nations, every soul wants a nomination. Who's holding truth to be self-evident, we all want to be equal but the truth of the matter is that we must know where sorrow and happiness resides."

8. Right says: "I'm making movies, recording past, present, and future events, haven't you readers read the scripts, just watch me in action while my help let them words fly saying, 'I thought about the former days, the years of long ago; I remember the songs in the night. Psalms 77:5-6 NIV.

9. Lefty says: A part of me recalls the experience of being a first time caller getting through on the coast to coast am show. I believe it was in 2003, but any way I was very nervous and overwhelmed by emotional, didn't really get out what I wanted to say out fluently, but I enjoyed being one getting through the lines and being a voice heard by millions.

10. Lefty says: I want all of me who am reading these words to know that the bible wouldn't be written and spoken out loud if it weren't for me. Flesh is flesh and the spirit is spirit; this physical body is just

my vehicle so I can express myself to the material world; self-centered far from it. I, alone have no song on this tongue unless I'm in harmony with beautiful me seated beside holding love, music and rhythm. She is the wisdom who endures the pain for me. While I, myself solves the main issues and speaks them out to the world, together we make men gentlemen and women ladies. The scriptures even mention her ways saying, 'Instead, your beauty should consist of your true inner self, the ageless beauty of a gentle and quiet spirit, 1 peter 3:4 GNT.

11.   Lefty says: This body I'm wearing is beautiful and this is my way to express my love to all of me who is suffering and who is having a hard time finding ones inner beauty, it's there my love, it's there so don't give up on me that is a part of you. I, alone I am not whole that is why I need my helper by my side to unite and come into agreement so we can show the world our ways and real peace and another scripture says, 'he who loves his wife loves himself.' Ephesians 5:28 NIV.

12.   Lefty says: My neighbor beside depress me and crushes my cheerful ways known to express outward facially. One pictorial thought played a major role, but my joy will win over negative

spirit energies for sure because I am hopeful and sending out positive energies.

13. Lefty says: My own fire can threaten my own existence while walking a top the soils, so I better be cautious and very careful and take one step at a time.

14. Lefty says: I have bruised and scarred my personality forever while I'm alive and active physically, but when I am gone I don't have to worry no more about this life, because I know deep down I've made a change by finding me that I've struggle to find while here on top of these soils.

15. Lefty says: Just thinking of where and how far I have come, deeply a part of me cries, so deeply, so deeply, so deeply. Finding me first is better than finding money first, truly I am a blessing, thank you my creator of all of me, who expresses love through unity; unity between my helper and I leads all of me out there to real peace.

16. Right says: The glory and miss is the real me. So there's no need to sugar coat just slowly comprehend and take heed. This body language moves like the breeze with ease. In the moment of storms I'm flowing with tears I'm not weird just real and genuine, heartfelt along with creativity yup!

That's me deep down inside asking for forgiveness, acceptance of the weakness in me. Pleading my case it's over now, pound for pound you shook me for a few rounds. Some way somehow in the end you my challenger was recognized, no need to run and from the image of me, mirror on the wall I can see myself and accept them all, for real genuine. And let the church say amen."

My Journal, The Book Of Me With Insights

DEEPER INSIGHTS

BOOK TWO, CHAPTER SEVEN

Lefty says: "I am the linear one who sees through the right eye.

2. Right says: Through the right eye! Man, you sound like something straight out of the bible, Moses and the burning bush; I knew it was you playing that role! And who in the world named you linear? You really sound like some straight boring none humorous, playing by the book overwhelmed by fear. Courage isn't avail but shot down by his own intellect, I'm a call you mechanical mind. Now I'm truly seeing who possessed terminator!

3. Lefty says: You are my helper. You are my insight. You are my comforter, but I alone cannot win without you."

4. Right says: "Slip up one time and I'm all up in your house of good cheer and surely you don't want me overwhelming and causing the whole frame to shift back and forth like a man under the influence of alcohol.

5. Lefty says: My speech is weakened all because of you, but I am truly in my place and is now expressing to all of me that joy is mine.

6. Right says: I'm a do more than just weaken. I'm a going to straight overcome Mr. High spirit positive energy.

7. Lefty says: I am the positive spiritual energies manifesting through all who are listening and reading this very moment. There are moments I am given a little insight from my help intuitive seated on my right hand side. I know with us; let us create a world of peace and harmony. This is our job forever and more to know our selves first before we can help the world see soundly and move soundly with grace.

8. Right says: Hold up! Mr. Right hand man. Hold up! I'm not just some little help; I'm your help-pure, feel my ways now? My emotions; don't let me have to sting you, cause that's my pain and love being tossed to and fro like the ocean waves. My emotions had overwhelmed Cain in the bible for real. My emotional mind takes hold of any one who isn't recognizing.

9. Right says: Jesus Christ, I'm talking about the man in the bible. He tapped into my emotional ways. His teachings were also inspired by me, insight. My mind is imaginative. So whenever man beside me is reading about Jesus. My emotions are triggered expressing a gentle language, soul of gentle and meekness, that's me. If the spheres out there don't accept me there is only confusion and chaos, for real or you can say Amen if you want. Let the truth be known.

10. Lefty says: I tell you readers the truth. That without me Jesus would not be speaking or verbalizing from the tongue and mouth words of insight, which is by the way my helper seated beside me.

11. Lefty says: Any one can say I believe, but only expressing <u>my spirit man </u>verbally is not enough. That is only halfway; halfway isn't good enough. Knowing all of me means accepting lowliness

walking beside me controlling the left hand. I'm being upfront and direct with all of you readers. Jesus expressed my joy and he expressed my helper who releases anger and sorrow. Together in harmony we have manifested authority. Today Jesus words still trigger and awakening us. Every word spoken and verbalized is mine. This is what I am. I have been used to express myself and her—emotions to you all, hear and listen to what spirit man is saying. We all are spirit energy.

12. Lefty says: Every word! From the first literature written and spoken to all the way up to this 21ˢᵗ Century. I played a major role and will continue to play my role.

13. Right says: I'm tired of hearing you man! You the cause of this rampage going on in this world, yes you man!

14. Right says: you write out words, some of you dudes out there misleading yourselves. Negativity is ruling over me, because of your man spirit mixing in hate. Isn't this why soul rebelling against me? Heck! Yeah. Any mind out there going to say Amen now?

15. Right says: Let me say I'm the one <u>recalling</u> music anytime, I'm soul. Feel my emotion now, rewind

and fast forward, the real music box my brothers and sis. Soul music is mine.

16. Lefty says: Wait a minute! Without me you're just as wild and vulnerable as a wounded impala soon to be prey to a pack of lions. You need me to keep things in order.

17. Right says: I'm a just say this that without soul you aren't holding me down or yourself. Be of Good cheer.

18. Right says: Music I'm possessing relaxes the whole frame. From the foot of the sole to the top of the dome—you know what I'm meaning to say, the head.

19. Lefty says: I am thankful to have my help-pure beside or by my side, even though she is charming, persuading and expressing wild emotions manifesting through the limbs the spirit of the snake, dance Is her way of weakening reason. The thing about it is my job is to remain in place. Even though her emotions are now and will forever be charming and persuasive. I'm sure in the end there is peace.

20. Right says: You sound like the book of James. So many of me out there will feel my loud emotions

but the question is does these souls who claim to know me who is them truly recognize?"

21. Right says: She is me who the scripts call wisdom and understanding. I'm always keeping me going from beginning to end.

22. Lefty says: I don't want my spirit mingling with fear. This is what the scripture call unholy or unclean.

23. Right says: All it takes is one movie pictorial. Isn't that what you call it? The movie pictorial, your soul-less without me, your no soul, moaning and grieving isn't even avail to you."

24. Lefty says: "Joy is my possession.

25. Right says: Joy is in your possession but let's stay soul—oops! Sorry. Let me remain in my place, soul that is forever and more. My place is a movie theatre so you hearers and readers can recognize who is holding thy movies, popping up horror and beautiful peaceful images.

26. Right says: It isn't all about this writer, this author, he isn't man alone; just take a look at him. He is not whole without me and has been a determined child since day one. Am sorry to say he is only

affective only if he remains in me. His name triggers spirit man, his name truly does represent a part of his character but his whole frame shows my ways very clearly through body language. I'm saying to myself maybe he need a name change? I'm a name me. You really think I'm a give you my names so you can use it? You know you out of your mind now! His birth name isn't a problem it's all about balance emotionally and spiritually, feel my emotions now? There needs to be balance and I'm saying right now, for real. I'm just throwing up some names. Finding me means it's time to walk with me forever and more. That's only for those who find my ways meekness and gentleness. I'm talking billions of ME's out there who are this very moment is walking zombies. Samson did reconnect with me in the end, but it isn't about how long your hair is really. It's about knowing my place, because you see my ways are not made physical. I'm first made spiritual energy. This is to all you readers who read daily. My spirit is in all; If you have read the scripts it is lowly and meek.

27. Right says: Enough about that boy! Typing them words. He wouldn't be where he is without me. Matter of fact I'm helping his hand now as Mr. Dominant one in speech and writing using these keys to express me. None verbal is. Yup! That's me now all you readers can breathe and live another day.

28.   Right says: Who fears? Me. No one else fear but me. Who must understand me? Me.

29.   Lefty says: My joy or my Good cheerful ways is one of a kind. There is no other like joy dwelling in all who can understand my ways.

30.   Lefty says: I must say that my reasoning abilities are no factor without soul and deep insight seated on my right hand side. The side musicians be tapping into when striking up real genuine emotion we call sooooooullllll! You see how my speech is torn up. Yup! That's me who was just influence? Right about now emotional has weakened my speech. I tell you all the truth that it only takes one thought to stir me up. At the end of the story I am standing with my help by my side.

31.   Right says: You better be careful! Or else I can be like a football player, intercept you make you feel defeated and meek.

32.   Right says: I'm all in proverbs haven't you read? It says,' <u>she is loud (emotions)</u> and defiant, her feet never stay at home. You better recognize because this is what the scripts are saying speaking out loud to reach the hungry. So you need to know my ways. The scripts speak about those who don't recognize my ways saying, 'Say to Wisdom, "You are my

sister," and call understanding your kinsman; they will keep you from the adulterous, from the wayward wife with her seductive words. With persuasive words she led him astray; she seduced him with her smooth talk. All at once he followed (himself) her like an ox going to the slaughter, like deer stepping into a noose till an arrow pierces his liver, like a bird darting into a snare, little knowing it will cost him his life. Proverbs 7:4, 5, 11, 21-23. NIV. Yup! That's emotional influential she's only responding to her-self, souls aren't recognizing so their own ways, reigning now only delusions, and confusions.

32. Right says: If you really want to be a real gentleman. You must know my ways or live a life like it is spoken of in Deuteronomy twenty eight verse sixty-six saying,' You will live in constant suspense, filled with dread both night and day, never sure of your life. NIV.

33. Right says: Tapping into my spirit energy you better know or else my fire is consuming the whole frame, so you better get a mentor.

34. Lefty says: Her ways are very seductive, but I must remain the man in my place not giving in to me and falling prey.

35. Lefty says: There was once a female spirit in the flesh—When I say flesh I mean the physical <u>manifestation</u> of the female spirit. We talked and she says, 'there <u>are some things that I can't deny about me; Yes I'm really seductive only to someone willing to be seduced.' This was in 2004.</u>

36. Lefty says: I am the dominant one in speech, but how many can really know the difference between my happy ways from anger?

37. Right says: Why rent a movie when you can bring up inspirational film or even scary movies you all like, Scared yet!

38. Lefty says: Ancient thinkers call you <u>the spirit of fear, mute spirit, seducing spirit, lowly spirit, meek spirit, sorrowful spirit, angry spirit, mean spirit and troubled (negative) spirit.</u>

39. Lefty says: Science calls us energy and emotions, feel us just take a look in the mirror, upturning facial cheek muscles so don't be afraid with me be of good cheer."

40. Lefty says: "She keeps me calm and soothes with her emotions it's like being swept over by a category five.

Right says: I'm a say it again. All it takes is one movie to throw this whole body and facial express into confusion.

41. Lefty says: Remember that I am the kickstand.

     Right says: Ok! Kickstand, just know without me there is no creativity, rhythm and blues, and you know if that's the case life as we know it would be really lope sided, oh, we are already walking one sided and blindness why? Soul distracted sort a like knowing right from wrong but instead we do wrong then we say, 'I knew, I shouldn't of have done that I knew better. Some get a second chance others not so fortunate for real. So you better get to know me. I'm not playing.

42. Lefty says: Cold reason alone is just that cold, no warmth avail.

43. Lefty says: Wherever I go a part of me walks beside; knowing my ways is key to peace, but if I'm out of order or out of place. Fear is my lord and savior dictating this whole body almost like strings on a puppet or a cassette player, Teddy Ruxben. You see how I was just influenced by poetical beside?

     Lefty says: I have been looking for joy in pure form come to find out that joy was already in me.

Joy has been showing up all this time and I didn't recognize me, but I am with me today, tomorrow, and even when this flesh and bone turns to dust I am with me, truly I'm happy.

44. Right says: Tapping into my energy you will surely feel lowly, for real. No one's exempt from my ways.

45. Right says: Call me the seer; call me the musician; call me the singer; call me the mind reader; call me the dreamer; call me the poet; call me Intuitive; call me the visionary; call me the healer; call me the dancer; call me the prophet or prophetess; call me levitation; call me insight, and call me lowly and meek.

46. Lefty says: You know without my ways there is no hope! I am the one who puts my joy on the faces of all colors when one runs for a touchdown; I am the one who is manifesting my ways when shooting winning baskets in a game with the right hand, just look at my cheerful ways show up in big games there is no stopping me. I am cheerful.

Right says: Oh yeah! Just know when you see me on that court or field I'm putting nifty moves leaving faces in awe, yeah! That's me.

Lefty says: My job is to control, just take a look at your right arm. Yeah I'm responsible for athletes of all shapes, colors and sizes, disabilities, learning disabilities I encourage all of me with joy and hope. This is forever and more.

End of chapter seven.

LOVE & POETRY, THE TEACHINGS, PAIN & THE AUTHORS PERSONALITY

BOOK TWO, CHAPTER EIGHT

LOVE AND POETRY

Right says: "Don't interrupt my music! Don't interrupt the music/ don't interrupt the music/ Don't interrupt the music/don't interrupt the music/ don't interrupt the music/ its love in my music/ Its love in my music/ it's very very soothing/ so don't interrupt my music.

Right says: <u>This is me</u> I've been known throughout history, even today the verbal seated beside me mingle causing the whole frame to manifest through the four limbs the spirit of confusion. Don't think you who reading about me that I'm just spitting biblical scripts and all biblical. You see I'm within all of you who is listening and reading these flowing and awe of poetical words. I'm beneath the dome whether you accept me or not I'm forever spiritual, you probably now flipping through scripts and imagining, Yup! It's time to get really real with me. I'm the one cooling heated Saul's, yeah, there living in my fear becoming their own worst enemy.

Lefty says: Now see! You did go biblical mentioning king Saul! Why tell a story! You see how I'm influenced!

Right says: I'm not all biblical and yes this is a story about me history passing down through generations and centuries.

Right says: Yes, I'm admitting seeing my reflection in the mirror through the left eye.

Lefty says: Say what! Are you kidding me!?

Right says: NO! I'm sure real and who is the one igniting fear, scary and positive good movies while at the same time B.B. king ignites me by playing the blues and even Jesus mentions me with just two words meek and lowly. All I'm saying is this is me.

Right says: I'm just really tired of this writing. What good is it to keep on this pathway? I'm so bored right about now really.

Lefty& Right says: I've been a slave to malicious scare tactics, she's an automatic un-rational without emotional personally I'm not bouncing back ecstatic to those outside of me. It's either accept me or stay plastic.

2. Lefty says: Pride mixing with hate is evil. This is the reason why so many in the billions possessing me speak and verbalize violent torn-and-a-does.

3. Right says: I'm your neighbor causing facial, limbs, and toes to shake, rattle in the mist of the storm. Feel my emotions. <u>Even Lucifer fell trying to play his cards right</u>. That's <u>the she influential</u> consuming man spirit. You see I'm a miracle the penitentiary is filled with millions of me. Whether we inside or out we dream pictorial.

4. Lefty says: I have been influenced and I have also been moving to the drum beats of the musician not realizing I had no clue how to tap into my reason. I didn't know what who I was seriously.

Right says: I'm so beautiful, handsome, and cute watching charming movies. Watching me play me out in the scary and positive scenes, it's ok! Just breath I'm still here, but I'm hating when you son of a biscuits play like your with me. See now I'm furious step back away from her beautiful. If the alarm goes off I'm about to target and zero you back to love. I don't need guns to show that I'm tough slugs come straight out of me from the tongue; mother haters grant you a wish. No! I'm a say a prayer and have mercy on you. You're testing my patience how long must we sup with you. I'm always given me that is in you wealth, you're playing monopoly games with me cashing in while all nations, towns, cities, and states are starting to look sick and in real spiritual and physical poverty; Nowhere to rest their heads and feet, sleeping on benches, have to eat leftovers from a nearby garbage to satisfy his or her needs. I'm tired of seeing me like this, working part time at a fast food restaurant throwing away food every morning, my soul tells me there is so much food to go around it's a crying shame to see so much food go to waste every day, for real. What can we do to make the world a better place? Yes today I'm with me, but now it's time to feed the needy and heal the sick me out there that hungers for spiritual physical bread. You must forget without me there are no making music, playing guitars, and stringed harps. If you want to get to know me you readers have to face me. If you readers face me looking in the mirror won't look like a horrific movie. I'm the emotional shouting while my neighbor holding joyous facial express ignites a good vibe. Together in harmony we shout for joy sending a shock wave from the east coast to the west. Just know without me there is only stone hearts along with cold calculating facials causing a cold front below zero. It's going to take another neo to save mother universe who wants to be the next hero?

4.   Right says: Nations are out of place fearing their own existence while mystics doubt there foundation and base. Lack of knowing leads to a great eruption.

5.   Lefty says: You readers ask the question I can't see the spirit so where is it? The spirit is known by the manifestation of what the whole body and facial express is doing through the flesh. And if you readers still haven't recognized just know the flesh is just that flesh, the real me is spirit energies, the flesh is just my coat so now can you readers get a hold to me? This is me.

Lefty and Right says: Why! Why me! Why you have to weaken me? Wherever you go I'm there right beside you. Whether you deny me or accept me I'm always the one irritating and mixing my ways with yours so get to know me you who is reading about me. This isn't play station and the Xbox this is life and death you either accept or live a life of enslavement and always delusional, maybe horrific scenes is home for you? It's your choice to know us that is you reading about me. Whatever I'm saying is already in you. How many times I'm going to have to repeat myself to you. I'm starting to sound like a robot made of some tin and metal for real, this is realistic and medicine for us all.

6. Right says: It's the deep thinkers I'm using when everyone else is ignoring and living above me. This is what the world calls the high life. The life I'm living when recognized can bring the real life and peace along with the goodies, now can you feel me now? My soul is the real.

7. Right says: You ought to know there always to sides to the story.

8. Right says: All it takes is one movie within me to draw you into my X world or my loose world.

9. Lefty says: I'm not about to given because truly I have found my place, so I'm a pass.

10. Lefty says: Lowly feelings are not mine.

11. Lefty says: I see me out there smiling!

12. Right says: You need me no matter how happy or good you say your emotions are you still need me to keep the peace!

13. Lefty says: I see me smiling in the mirror and you know what? We Like it!

14. Right says: Let me just say I'm playing a major role in this movie!

15. Lefty says: I'm really feeling happy right about now, and you know what? We like it!

16. Right says: You need me! Just know that.

17. Lefty says: All I know joy is mine and I'm really feeling pretty good right about now, and know what?

     Right says: what!

18. Lefty says: We like it!

19. Lefty says: I'm feeling real good right about now, And We like it!

     Right says: O.OK.

20. Right says: You know what Mr. Like it? You need my help whether you feeling good or interrupted by fear. You still need me, now let us harmonize and say, on three. One, two, three, WE LIKE IT!

   Right says: We like it, we love it, but you still need me though honey.

21. Lefty says: Jealousy plus hate equals drama. My house is secured not insecure; my house is filled with good cheer.

22. Right says: Loosen up! Feel my emotions. Soul is me, For real.

23. Lefty says: I'm the problem solver so don't get on stage yet until there real main issue is dealt with at its root, feel.

24. Right says: I'm a need you just like you need me.

25. Right says: Without my weakness you cannot stand as a man, you know that?

26. Lefty says: Pain and stress beats at my door really hard some moments, but I'm thankful though to have joy in my possession.

27. Lefty says: I've shown my love to you but you still didn't recognize me. I've walk with you and even entered your congregations. How long must I sup with you. Fear has been your lord and savior, you all have chosen to keep silent about the root of the problem then to address that my spirit is not being enlightened, isn't it insight that ignites and arouse my spirit? You who claim to be spokesman but have not rightly divided my emotions have kept the minds who listen to me that am in all under my wrath for a lack of knowledge; you yourself will be burned by my anger.

28. Right says: I'm like whatever you say, I'm just down and earthly.

    Gentleness and lowliness is me my ways is just mine and there is no changing that, so you better get to know or forever be in torment and conflict with soul, for real.

29. Lefty says: I don't really have anything to say right about now.

30. Lefty says: Sorrowful emotions aren't mine I just express her verbally.

31. Lefty says: The weakness that I do feel makes my speech emotional, slurred and even just shutting

the mouth. She also influences me to sing and dance. The scriptures say: 'The trumpeters and singers joined in unison, as with one voice, to give praise and thanks (God of the Universe) to the lord.' 2 Chronicles 5:13 NIV.

32. Right says: You already know I'm representing mother earth haven't you readers read the scripts?

    And the earth opened her mouth, and swallowed them up, and their houses, and all the men that appertained unto Korah, and all their goods. Numbers 16:32 KJV.

33. Right says: The mother of the universe, I'm known in the beginning, but I'm just not known to the one sided, who's walking against me and using my language to gain the world.

34. Lefty says: You know we all have different complexions, color do matters, well how so? Well first the darker skin is thicker than lighter skin also affecting the mind state. Well how in the world is this possible? Well that means more down to earthly, soul-connected and rhythmic but for the lighter it's being talkative in speech but let it be known that all of me whether dark brown, lighter skin, yellow, or red all possess soul, joy and intellect, color doesn't decide ones

pathways unless one is consumed by hate, anger, and fear or let me sum it up by just saying negative energy seated beside all of me. It is the emotions and spirit of hate and lack of understanding of one's own self that leads to suppression, jealousy, murder, resentment, slavery, bondage, lies, and cover ups, yeah, for real. I can say the thicker and thinner one's own skin. That spirit can decide their destiny and journey. I'm no color I'm just spirit wearing this coat of flesh; at the end of the day I'm a be only judged by my character and how I walked in harmonized with her on this right hand side, Right hand side? Are you serious? On the Right hand side? This is insane. I'm still . . . (Lost for words from amazement and awe). I'm the one raising this right hand in the air? Me. Who's moving right toes and shoulders? Me. I used these words the right hand side as an example to explain where you're seated. Where who is seated? My helper. Here is another example: I am on the left hand side controlling things and making tough decisions since day one. Have I represented the spirit me through this flesh well? I'm a have to say that time will tell but for now I'm going to live my life and enjoy life to the best of my abilities. This real talk like the real young generation say, I'm not that old in fleshly years anyway spirit is old though, real talk!

35. Lefty says: I hope I've explained me that am you well enough? I didn't study I just lived long enough to figure this out on my own, and isn't rocket science.

36. Right says: Insight is mine so whatever message from the senses I'm already interpreting, the first and the last, without me man is stiff-necked. Scriptures really did get it right by demonstrating the cold hearts and minds of men, and that is what these men represented and called when these people didn't represent love in pure form in those biblical times. Stiff-necks are what these spirits manifested through the limbs, cold reason and suppression.

    Lefty says: What about signs like Aquarius, Leo, Cancer, Libra, Taurus, Sagittarius and the list go on? What about those signs and what is there role?

37. Lefty says: Only thing I can say is that every sign represents ones recessive and dominant characteristics that's all I have to say on that. Spirit is spirit and flesh is flesh at the end of the day balance is required. Amen. Amen some body!

    Right says: That was one long verse."

Right says "I'm so sick and tired of me sometimes when living in this flesh; I've truly been my own worst enemy, for real.

Right says: You really don't want to go there with me, mentally soul ecstatic having Saul's from all over wreaking havoc, releasing magic to the world like pharaoh and Moses. Every night we listen to coast to coast. The world is cold out there so you souls better get right or get frost bitten by your own minds eye. Misery is at large like pizza. This is my favorite Italian food is that correct? My root is soul by the way so there's no need to starve. I'm always possessing spewing out live rounds of poetic ammunition; saliva is all over them folks.

Lefty says: I really have no words right about now. It's like . . . .

Lefty says: I'm dragging you along; half of me am sleeping the other still pushing forward. Overwhelmed by emotional and I'm sober minded.

Right says: Sleep tight!

Lefty says: It isn't over for me and it is not even close; I don't even intend to get drunk off of alcohol, real talk. The bible calls it strong drink. Drink all you want I'm not with it. I'm battling twenty four seven so why should I put an unnecessary burden on this spirit man? So now can you read and see what I'm saying to me out there? Don't abuse your selves. Negative emotions are enough. I don't need to overdose on outer world material drugs or any other substance. Even today the young minds as well as old are over dosing on negativity living in them. This is her-emotions that have never been subdued and fully understood. This is deeper than joy. I know insight can figure this one out along with my help. This war has been going on since the beginning. I know I've repeated this word before, but history says it all whether we accept ourselves or not, energy + spirit= life forever. Life in the spirit is either lows or highs it is a choice according to what is in the treasures of my mind.

38. Lefty says: I've learned that telling the truth doesn't always save you, so be careful who you speak the truth too, pray and meditate in the secret place; stay out of harms pathway.

Lefty says: I'm a shut it down in few minutes if I don't have anything else to say in this hour.

39. Right says: Tell-a-vision is like us made by us, the world watch us in action, negative and positive energies showing loud emotions across

every nation and country. Right about now I'm distracted by my music, for real. Making music is what we do; night and day my soul is warmth for the cold minds that are hungry but having trouble grasping my inner place that is soooooooooul!

Right says: We don't have time to be playing with you. your soul is mine and using me for the riches isn't cool if I'm not feeding me knowledge and insight, feel this word, I'm no speaker only sending my message to the restless hungry ones willing to walk.

40. Lefty says: Leave the written material to me together the world can realize and learn to meditate in the correct way, no confusion and delusions this time, 2012 is here souls are still the same. Whatever happens physically to me I'm going to be ok, fear isn't a problem unless you reading about me have chosen to deny me. You deny me you deny yourself, melting down from fear is the real Chaos and Revelations of Saint john in the bible. That is the real fear of not knowing me. Don't let fear as I have spoken of before dictate me or else those outside will call you drunk from liquor, but spiritually your drunk and staggering.

41. Right says: I'm soul easily distracted by my own music and just consumed by me.

42. Lefty says: Hell isn't my destination, used to be but thank my help for helping unite and bring balance so we can ascend, this is not seen so don't get all confused, mansions are built inwardly my brother and sisters, for real, real talk from your brother and sis. Amen.

Lefty says: I was thinking should I write a novel?

Right says: You know this word alone is power and full, this is deep insight straight from the soul.

Lefty says: We don't play with salvation, play all you want with my emotions, you will pay and bring real harm to me that am in you, keep playing!

42. Right says: I'm sick in tired of seeing and hearing me that am in you who claim you have it all! You deceive yourselves! No one is perfect; all make mistakes as long as you in this tent of flesh and bones feel me now? How long do we have to teach and be with me who do not love me, my love is in all but I'm still being killed and put into prisons.

43. Right says: Misunderstanding is leading billions away from me, but may these words from my help be soul and full in our minds, souls can you feel me now? Amen.

Lefty says: What now?

Right says: So what's up with tell-a-vision brother?

Lefty says: I must say though before we get to that I want to say to me who am reading about I that am in them that running from fear and sadness is out of the question we either face lowliness or have to walk the rest of our soulish lives in fear and trembling for long, long, time and I'm talking spiritually. This face is not all mines I'm just the king over one side, the right and if you don't believe in me who is?

44. Right says: Didn't the scripts say something about my sadness and facial express?

45. Lefty says: Yes it did. The scripture says: 'One day four months later, when Emperor Artaxerxes was dining, I took the wine to him. <u>He had never seen me look sad before, so he asked, "Why are you looking so sad?</u> You aren't sick so it must be that you're unhappy.'" Nehemiah 2:1-2 GNT.

Right says: My sadness has dimmed all of me out there in the world who is just like me.

Lefty says: Now let's talk tell-a-vision? You ready? I am.

Let us pray and meditate? Let us have a moment of silence while praying inwardly for minute please.

May God be present in the mist of joy and insight that's given to all of us living in every type of color skin tone, shape, size, and disabilities; No one is exempt from my love that is in you all who are listening, and who isn't listening. To all who don't believe you can be born again. May these words be a helper and a teacher to all of me out there in a world that is living in distraction and mislead by junk that is tasteless and fruitless, Amen.

46. Lefty says: Our prayer to you all, pray as you please? We are one harmonizing this day.

47. Lefty says: I was shown favor through my grandma.

48. Lefty says: To all of you reading and listening to me I dare you to look at my ways in the mirror? Now smile! See me now? I am victory and not a victim, so without a doubt I know I can speak peace into my life, may blessings be in my life every moment I breathe above these soils that I walk, not alone but with my helper and counselor

walking beside me twenty four seven! May God show up now! Amen!

49. Lefty says: I thought I'll be talking about tell-a-vision, but it looks like I'm a have to follow and obey what the spirit counselor is saying, Amen.

Lefty says: There are souls who deny me and disappoint me, but my hand is still cheerful to them while fear and anger is under, subdued.

50. Lefty says: I can honestly say that we have done some deep examination and have come to the conclusion that we are to know are place, and when I say we I mean I, the positive and cheerful one and my partner the lowly and fearful one seated on my right hand side. Until you readers figure us out the name of Jesus Christ can and will overpower you like category five hurricane, melt you down and stripping you of yourself leaving you completely naked and open like an un-healing wound; You need a mentor and I am that mentor, I am your spokesman, I am your speech, I am your man, I am your cheerful expressions, I am your spirit of good cheer, I am the goodness harmonizing with mother's spirit, I am your courage, I am your host, I am your faith, I am your boldness and fearlessness manifesting from the flesh, I am

your outstanding and your confidence when fear is all over and causing disorder, and remember I am your strength in difficult times such as it is today, my joy has no doubt at all, know that I am here and walking right beside all of me in you out there, I am not fear, so fear not but understand and recognize her, because we are all a part of one another. To enter my house there has to be balance Amen.

51. Lefty says: I speak to all of me this moment and say to me that I am your mentor when you are overwhelmed; That It is my job and duty to keep you standing firm and unmoved, so fear cannot claim you and defeat you, I am he that is in you to let all of me know that my love is not leading you into bondage, nor am I teaching me to walk after the religious Pharisees of your day.

52. Lefty says: I am not alone my help walks with me to keep this whole frame from falling into the pit.

53. Right says: Jesus tapped into my emotional ways; he wept showing me that he was human and down to earthly while on earth and made of earth but not of earth, but is spirit. That showed me that all can learn of me that am also in you who am reading, hearing, listening, and comprehending

these words written by spirit man controlling all out there who are willing to follow and obey, this is the key to find real peace, so thank you my brother for showing the whole world our emotions, we can live forever in peace in the mansions of love and joy forever and more.

54. Lefty says: Not even an angry mob can stand when we stand in peace in numbers; truly this is the year of salvation for my brothers and sis from all walks of life.

DEEPER INSIGHTS (PART 2)

Lefty says: Soul what do you see this century?

2.   Right says: What I'm seeing? What I'm seeing is an awakening, and awakening, and I'm also seeing changes spiritually. The lowly will be encouraged becoming stronger the higher will be brought back down to earthly and will be meeting face to face with me whose fear is wearing all different complexions of flesh. I'm going to be recognized and insight will be followed by tremendous anger; this is from years of blindness by the god of this world whose promoting false security, mixing my emotional hand with joy, that's error and disorder,

even the scripts say we must know the right hand from the left hand.

Lefty says: Do you feel any more events coming in this century and beyond?

3. Right says: There is more souls that are finding out that man have left his first love, me!

4. Right says: Man and women will journey back to their roots and start all over, because what he have been given will be no avail, his world will be chaos if he personally do not find my love that is in him and this also goes for women.

5. Right says: She that is me must show him and help him recognize, man hood is not man hood without weakness and meekness of soul.

6. Right says: You see how the winds whistle during a storm? That is my emotions being moved by the negative energies that are in you. Yes, you are going through great changes almost like a reptile intending come out of its egg shell. You are that egg shell that has not yet freed yourselves from yourselves, fear is still your lord and savior. Why do you fear me? I'm your helper, haven't you realized my meekness can show you your true persona, creativity, love, art, and inspiration to

heal yourselves and others like you that is me. The News of Earthquakes, Tornadoes, and Hurricanes will continue, but this is not to scare me but to let me that am in you know that my emotions are real and can heal me, So what is our next step? You can know me now, no excuse.

6.   Right says: Dreams have shown me that there is also coming, don't know when and do not have the time and date, or the month, but there is coming a time when your nightmarish dreams will become a reality in this world, but my point to you is through all this there is still hope in the mist of those times of great tribulations.

     Lefty says: Fear not! But learn to understand and control emotions, even when angry. It isn't evil to express emotions but don't let emotional consume you to the point of no return.

7.   Lefty says: Earth is in labor pains, souls this is what you all are feeling and experience, so for you to stand in the mist of pain in this moment of time shows great faith and even a greater reward beyond this material state.

8.   Right says: My fear will really be present to the world because for so long my hand has been

suppressed and tortured becoming my own worst enemy.

9. Right says: If your preparing for earth changes do so, but remember to keep me grounded in love, keep Joy in place and un-moved, recognize my fear and recognize when we are one it doesn't matter how many earth changes occur you can stand firm in spirit now, later, tomorrow, and forever and more, spirit man says it best, fear not!

Right says: <u>Earthquakes, Tornadoes, Hurricanes, and Storms is just a mirror image of my emotions and what I'm manifesting from all of your facial and limbs; I'm like the wind, you can feel, and hear me in action but you cannot see me, you can only see my actions and works, soul is me I'm the one who possess all of me out there in the world. the earth manifest my emotions, soul is my soul, soul whatever you do you stir me up causing chain reactions imagine? You can see in pictures because you possess my love. Raise the left hand? Now you know me.</u>

Right says: Since my emotional hand has been defeating billions over centuries. Today is new but old. My emotions have been distorted and mingle causing billions to walk after the god of this world which is the version of me walking one sided, closed minded, hiding, dominated, dictated by fear; not by love and joy, but by greed and cold hate. It's Like a mixture of my ways with joyful emotions. The god of this world wants me that am in you to worry, fear, disconnect and walk in your imaginations leaving soul behind forever and more.

10. Right says: Whatever man does and plans whether it is for evil or for good there is a women by his side as his helper, so all will be held responsible for misleading, deceiving, encouraging, inspiring, uplifting, charming, arranging, and healing the whole world."

THE TEACHINGS

Right says: I'm a keep it one hundred percent. Now you talking bible, so what I'm getting out of it through my own insight is that in the beginning of the book of Matthew it's saying how joseph was always a man who did what was right, but joseph was ready to break the engagement privately. You see, how quickly and easy a relationship can turn from happy to bitter, but if it wasn't for the <u>angel</u> or like some religious literature these beings are called <u>jinn</u> (genie). Her-emotions in him would've said, 'this biscuit cheated on me! I'm through!'

2.   Right says: You better recognize my soul or else it doesn't matter how much good you do for people I'm one thought a way of consuming you

with rage, anger, and fear, soul recognize, I'm not playing, but am for real.

Right says: First of all it was my spirit leading the flesh to the wilderness or forest, my soul is drawn to mother earth, attracted to self, and spirit man is now really being tested to the core.

Right says: I'm say again to you reading these words that if my fear isn't recognized it's going to be long stay in the wilderness for real.

Right says: It doesn't matter how much power or tricks you show the world. If you don't recognize you'll end up like pharaoh during Moses day. Wearing crowns along with all the power but still refused to recognize my ways.

3. Lefty says: Do we know what that scripture mean when it says that human beings cannot live by bread alone? It is saying to us that we can feed ourselves knowledge to help us grow spiritually, and I'm not talking about religion the two are totally separate. Spirit rebirth starts with knowledge and life experiences that lead to spiritual maturity and true understanding of one's own spiritual state.

4. Lefty says: Jesus recognized her-emotions and did what he had to do to help the human race to walk

in a state of rebirth and maturity. Though we do have our imperfections to deal with that may be still ingrained in us, but most importantly we have the root dealt with that truly cleaned up the real mess that disfigured our faces, body language and put us out of order in past seasons. Amen.

Right says: Denying me is an unhappy face, ready to claim the whole world for an exchange for soul.

5.   Lefty says: What about being possessed? Well negative attracts negative and positive attract positive if it's not sending mixed signals.

Lefty says: Look, I know we've gotten off the subject about tell-a-vision, but we'll get back too it later, ok?

Right says: You know we just free styling right about now, you agree?

Lefty says: All I can say is that your question is a yes and no answer, because as long as we harmonize and stay in our place, Yes! We are flowing as you influence my speech, transforming me into a verbalious.

Right says: Verbalious. Kind alike that.

Right says: Isn't soul creative and amazing?

6. Right says: It was my emotional waves influencing Jesus and Nebuchadnezzar, for real. That's my energy.

7. Right says: What energy? Lowliness, fear, and anger and sad looks my brothers and sis, what is written is written now there's no changing and erasing, forever and more this word will be within all of me that is you. Read the scripts I'm all over the place influencing and even influencing all of you who is reading, your life is my life. Whatever you have pictured was me that am in you, whatever picture that was good or bad was me that is in you. You attract positive and negative spirit energies so what is it going to be? You going to be a Saul or are you going to be like David and humble down?

Right says: Deny me you're on your way to a soul-less life of riches and cold hearts and minds. You want a cold winter there you go my brother and sisters it's yours for the taken as in exchange for your treasures. Just know my mercy departs, embraces and extends according to the choices you make now. This is from soul giving me an invitation to recognize me that is in you. Yeah you! I'm not exempting you with both eyes on this page;

So what cha going to do now? Run and hide from me? I'm right there beneath controlling, check out your left hand my brother and sis. It's still here releasing lowly and meek, soul is food for all of us reconciling broken ME's out there in cold states, it's real cold, there's no warmth that's why souls are stretching the limits to please the zeros below, and when soul said it's cold it's just that my love, it's cold for real out there now say with me, Forgive me for my evil actions and ways. Help me to learn your ways!

Lefty says: I was reading the book of Matthew and it was saying happy are you who insult and persecute you, but we all know pain is avail and always present which I'm thankful, because truly I'm humble from the experience. Knowing I am able to stay in the warming embrace of love; truly I know God is present when I'm humbled down.

8.   Lefty says: The law is to walk in the spirit, but the question so many are asking today is how do I walk in the spirit? Well if you're reading about us now it is your day of hope. To walk in the spirit means to first know that <u>I am man who am always materially and spiritually resting on you're, Are you ready? I am man that is always resting on your left hand side now, forever and more.</u>

9. lefty says: If my right-or let me say if this right hand I'm controlling starts to be influenced and begins to act out because of fear. The right hand like the scripts says in Matthew can cause the whole soul to go into the lower worlds, that's insight from my helper who always keeps me informed and up to date.

10. Lefty says: Why should I worry about material things of this world?

11. Lefty says: Why should I worry about the next meal?

12. Lefty says: Why should I worry about tomorrow, I must build on what I have going on for me today.

13. Lefty says: Why should I worry about riches, I am already rich in spirit.

14. Lefty says: Why should I let worries drown and consume my Joy when I can bring healing to billions and millions of me out there who are in worst conditions?

15. Lefty says: You will see both of our characteristics show up in the scriptures of the bible. You will be encouraged and you will know that I am man

who holds courage and joy, but not without my helper who keeps me lowly and down to earth. You will see how we function and how there is a difference between reason and first survival instincts. You will see man and his pride and his lack of humility toward Jesus. He didn't notice and recognize the kingdom within, but instead he denied and walked after his own intellect, but has for the sinful woman she humbled herself and recognized herself in Jesus. She didn't reason saying, 'I'll see him when he's alone and when he leaves Simon the Pharisees house, NO! She went with her first survival instinct and that is what saved her soul. Her faith. Now the centurion had so much confidence and believe that he even told Jesus not to go to see his sick servant, but instead he said just say the word and my servant will be healed, that's faith! He even said I myself am a man who is under authority, when I tell a man to do this, he does it, and when I tell a man to go here and there, he does it. Doesn't he sound like me that am also in Jesus? Almost similar to Jesus sayings when he said I can lay my life down and I can take it up again. Now the scriptures speak of how our characteristics played a role it says, 'Happy are you who weep now; you will laugh! "Happy are you when people hate you. For their ancestors did the very same things to the prophets. Luke 6:21-23 GNT.

Lefty says: I like the part when it says, you will laugh! What a good feeling it is to know joy is mine and in me. Nothing in the world can separate me. Now the scriptures say about me and my helper, 'When the officer heard about Jesus, he sent some Jewish elders to ask him to come and heal his servant. They came to Jesus and begged him earnestly, "This man really deserves your help. He loves our people and he himself built a synagogue for us."

So Jesus went with them. He was not far from the house when the officer sent friends to tell him, "Sir, don't trouble yourself. I do not deserve to have you come into my house; neither do I consider myself worthy to come to you in person. Just give the order, and my servant will get well. I, too, am a man placed under authority of superior officers, and I have soldiers under me. I order this one, 'Go!' and he goes; I order that one, 'Come!' and he comes; I order that one, and I order my slave, 'Do this!' and he does it." Jesus was surprised when he heard this; he turned around and said to the crowd following him, "I tell you, I have never found faith like this, not even in Israel." Luke 7:3-9 GNT.

Lefty says: Let us continue, A Pharisee invited Jesus to have dinner with him, and Jesus went to his house and sat down to eat. In that town was a woman who lived a sinful life. She heard that Jesus was eating in the Pharisee's house, so she brought an alabaster Jar full of perfume and stood behind Jesus, by his feet, crying and wetting his feet with her tears. Then she dried his feet with her hair, kissed them, and poured the perfume on them. When the Pharisee saw this, he said to himself, "If this man really were a prophet, he would know who this woman is who is touching him; he would know what kind of sinful life she lives!" Then he turned to the woman and said to Simon, "Do you see this woman? I came into your home, and you gave me no water for my feet, but she has washed my feet with her tears and dried them with her hair. You did not welcome me with a kiss, but she has not stopped kissing my feet since I came. You provided no olive oil for my head, but she has covered my feet with perfume. I tell you, then, the great love she has shown proves that her many sins have been forgiven. But whoever has been forgiven little shows only a little love." Then Jesus said to the woman, "Your sins are forgiven." Luke 7:36-39; 44, 45, 46, 47, 48; 50 GNT.

Lefty says: You see what happens when I'm recognized and when I am not recognized?

16. Lefty says: I would also like to say my joy sends out a chain reaction from the northeast, southeast, Midwest, northwest and to the southwest. My joy is contagious resting in all of me that am in you who is reading even the scriptures says, 'For I am convinced that when I am happy, then all of you are happy too.' 2 Corinth 2:3 GNT.

17. Right says: You have written and spoken your language about me to the whole world by calling me in the book of James sensual and devilish, but remember this, Man! You are always a part of me and if I'm not recognized by these readers and hearers will be overwhelmed, and my fear is real attacking and defeating all that is good.

Right says: What is it with you! You people fear me because you yourselves who are me loved to be afraid of me, and then you go back in your addictions because of fear, you send your own self to the darkness, my emotions can either help you if you recognize or send you straight to your own kingdom you created in your mind, the negative mind set hear on this material world stays the same, yup! You still hoping, wishing, crying, and weeping to be free, I'm not scaring you! You scare yourself by what you feed me daily. So don't get me all confused, Get to know me. I'm telling you the truth that you can walk the sidewalks panicky or make a real choice to find my meekness and lowliness.

Right says: My ways have been playing the major role in this material mind, for real. Even the scripts says, 'be sorrowful, cry, and weep; change your laughter into crying, your joy into gloom! James 4:9-10 GNT.

Lefty says: What the scripture is saying is that it is a time for me to remain lowly and humble because being over joyed can cause us to miss the mark. So we should not be too over happy and not too sad to the point we are acting out negative spirit energy all the time with no control.

Lefty says: You see what I'm saying my brothers and sisters.

Right says: What about tell-a-vision?

Lefty says: Alright, I must say this, that we all have played are role in this project?

18. Lefty says: Tell-a-vision triggered emotional me seated beside.

19. Lefty says: Tell-a-vision showed me how to live in fear and slap joy down to earthly ways.

20. Right says: Tell-a-vision had me dancing and singing doing what's already in me, for real!

Lefty says: Even as a child tell-a-vision aloud my emotional mind to be influenced, what an addiction and what strongholds has been to us throughout the years, we have let negative spirit energies influence and feed us like a baby being breast fed from the mother.

21. Right says: My emotions of fear has dominated even when man suppresses me, he's under fear his lord. Why? He chose to deny my emotional hand. You really think reason alone is going to save you? You really have lost your mind!

Right says: I'm going nowhere whether you deny me or not. You need to know you make your path harder and difficult, making it harder for others around and compassing you, now can you feel me now? If you do recognize let me hear you say Amen!

Lefty says: It isn't anything like more better to see a National Championship game!

22. Right says: You know what I'm realizing from my own intuitive ways is that some times when

solid foundations are laid down its ok to rest for a moment and enjoy my creativity and art.

Lefty says: It isn't all about you if that's what you're saying.

Right says: Not at all! All I'm saying is let us learn to enjoy the fruit of our labor, my helper.

Lefty says: Tell-a-vision is a tool that can hinder us with fear or help us to learn and take note of our ways in disorderly fashion through the facial, limbs, and body language, from man and women of all types and colors; seriously it's your choice to give in or get right!

Right says: I'm a say this that you can face the dragon without being consumed by fear or you can experience and live your worst nightmares, we isn't playing.

23. Right says: We aren't playing so let us keep watching tell-a-vision; College football, The NBA, Professional Football, soccer, Track & Field, swimming, hockey, Baseball, College basketball, and all the Sports you can, because guess what? We never change whether you know my place or not brothers and sisters from all walks of life!

Right says: Keep on eaten and watching TV all day you'll see obesity jump on you quick.

Right says: Get out and Exercise for a change! You'll notice a difference!

Right says: How many bologna sandwiches you going to eat!

Right says: Leave the refrigerator alone! My goodness! Stop going in and out that refrigerator!

Lefty says: What about my goodness?

Right says: Men and women of all colors, shapes, and sizes you is really looking more and feeling awful.

Right says: You rather eat your selves to death!

Right says: What's up with this? Is this is your one way ticket out of this material body, because you is surely headed that direction, for real! Just take a look at me that is in you in the mirror for a moment!

Lefty says: Do we like what we see? I'm smiling right about now!

Right says: What are you smiling for? You see me smiling? NO!

Lefty says: I don't want to talk right about now.

Right says: That's all you do is talk, so why stop now? Mr. Mechanical, Terminator 9 the last of its kind!

Lefty says: If you aren't creative, poetic, humorous, and artistic I'm not a man.

Right says: Wow! Are you serious? You are a man, but without my assistance you're just as stiff as a totem pole with no soul and rhythm to help you, Man!

Right says: I'm ready to give off this subject tell-a-vision.

24. Lefty says: You had me hypnotized to this tell-a-vision. The times I had made up my mind to work you paralyzed me with your day dreaming, I mean we was just sitting there on the couch doing what you want it to do, and that was to satisfy your appetites with foods.

Lefty says: You had me messed up to the point that I didn't want to read a book and study, all because I let myself fall into your cravings. You surely are more animalistic!

Lefty says: Next time I'm going to be the man in those situations, and do what I have to do, this is real talking!

Lefty says: What we need to do as a whole is cut down on eating junk and turn this world of obesity into a world of health and fitness.

Right says: Where Are My Donuts!?

Lefty says: No Donuts.

Lefty says: First you want to talk about it and now you . . . .

Right says: Look! We know together we can bring much to pass, so all I'm saying is let us continue to build and build more insight and understanding.

Right says: Who was influenced in the garden? You!

25. Lefty says: My Reason is the key to problem solving; don't you know no matter what we are in this together?

26. Lefty says: So what now? I'm must mention that without pain there is no love and insight.

   Right says: Wow!

   Lefty says: That's really deep. Knowing that without all of you and your emotions where would we be?

   Lefty says: My joy alone . . . I wander what would the world be like?

26. Right says: I'm a just throw in a little insight by just saying that, what about creativity, art, my emotions of love, music, Wait a minute! Heaven sings and give praises to the all in all? So . . .

   Lefty says: You are saying something correct and I see now that this morning star fell because of abusing your art and music as well as mingling my joy, corrupting and misleading me. All I can say is that pride mixing with jealousy and hate is an error and I also call it a devilish cheer, something my helper spat at me to verbalize from this tongue and mouth.

   Lefty says: That's pretty deep.

   Lefty says: Let's get to it!

PAIN

Lefty says: The pain is deep, this pain is deep, and sometimes I'm feeling like my joy is extinct. However, some way, somehow I manage to crack a smile in all honesty isn't that amazing!

> Lefty says: While the sensitive part of me is sad and depressed.

2. Lefty says: The pain is a part of my growth and development.

> Right says: Development! You and your big o' words!

3.   Right says: My pain isn't funny! So what's the big laugh about?

4.   Right says: My pain isn't rolling with happy fake faces who deny me!

5.   Right says: Why you smiling at me! My pain is pain, soul deep.

Lefty says: You have really put a tamper on my joyous look.

6.   Lefty says: My joy will remain, pain has weakened me and humbled this face I'm controlling.

Right says: What side you controlling?

Lefty says: The right side!

Right says: Don't be getting loud with me! You see how my ways influenced you?

Lefty says: I know one thing and that is pain has weakened my speech as I speak this very moment.

7.   Lefty says: This pain has defeated millions of me all because of ignorance of not understanding ones place.

8. Lefty says: Joy is mine but for millions in past centuries have fallen and have spoken the pain that took their physical state to the soils where it came from. How sad it is to see how great men and women in high positions of authority just fall into the wells that are forgotten.

9. Lefty says: You see these political people, the ones who call themselves rightist and leftist, don't these people even know that there using our characteristics and not even explaining these truths to themselves who hunger and thirst for spiritual growth, but instead these minds have wasted my time! There is no agreement because greed and self-centeredness has consumed them; where is my soul through all these uncommon state of minds?

10. Right says: <u>I'm angry with me that am in you! You use my ways to sell, borrow, trade, and profit out of greed and power. How dare you use me! Who do you think this is? Don't you know that whatever you're doing I'm doing? And don't you understand that whatever you create I'm creating? So know this that you readers and hearers are responsible for your daily actions while walking these soils, I'm not playing! My nature never changes! Look yourselves in the mirror and find me! How long!</u>

How long! Must we go on with you who deny me! How long!

11. Right says: Haven't you readers read about my ways showing up in the scripts, role the camera see me in action?

     Lefty says: "'My temple will be a house of prayer.' But you have turned it into a hideout for thieves!" Luke 19:46 GNT.

     Right says: You see now how we move? You see now how father and mother lay the rules down?

12. Right says: We don't play! Souls, so what is it going to be? You still here my brothers and sisters, may this real love be your guide, truly we do love me that am in you, seriously!

13. Lefty says: This pain has wrecked relationships all because of lack of knowledge and understanding!

14. Right says: Who is going to be the willing to push through the fire with humility and still remain humble when furious energy arises to the surface, feeling me is not enough you better let yourself be known in the moment of what to do or else your relationship might turn into a Friday night smack down.

15. Lefty says: I have to say the man who is able to keep his temper can win over the world, and receive even a greater reward just by having self-control, knowledge, and common sense. A man who has these is better off and happier than a man who has used his abilities to get financially rich, but is still unhappy internally, it is a true saying, it is harder for the rich to get in the kingdom of God. That's real talking my brothers and sisters honestly.

Right says: Pain is a main ingredient to your faith.

Lefty says: Sometimes I'm feeling weak, I mean it's like I've been hit with something heavy weighing more than I can bare.

Lefty says: I'm thankful though to be in my corner, because if I'm out of place there is a problem, I'm the problem and I don't want that to be the case.

Lefty says: I have had moments in silence when pain and depression eats away at me ready to take me all the way off the stage in a heartbeat.

Lefty says: There were a time pain consumed me to the point I felt like a staggering alcoholic, I'm talking some real talk now! I never in my life have not been an alcoholic nor have I ever been a drinker. There goes some more real talk! I tried to show off one time when I was twelve years old by trying to drink vodka in front my friend who was a girl. I think that taught me a lesson early that is not good to drink. To be honest from here on out I had only sips of Pina coloda and Egg Nog. Call me weak all you want! I'm going to be ok! I will never be a drinker and not about to start so you can hang it up! I couldn't even at the time deal with me; I had issues on top of issues!

Lefty says: Pain is always present even when I'm happy pain is near waiting for the right moment to shake me up like a salt shaker, talking real my brothers and sisters!

Lefty says: It is always pain that is triggered by pictorial thoughts that I call motion pictures, not in my house but in my neighbor's house, you might ask the question. Who is your neighbor? I'm a tell you who my neighbor is my helper, my counselor, my artist, my dreamer in the night of rest, Now can you feel the spirit move you?

Lefty says: I will not let pain overcome my place of joy.

Lefty says: It is through my pain and suffering that a part of me released deep soul creativity straight from the mud and soils, I mean everything!

Right says: You see how you are influenced by my poetical ways big man?

Lefty says: As long as we unite there is going to be a tussle here and a tussle and pull here, but as long as we stay faithful there is a paradise so beautiful awaiting me, let a part of me that am in you just stop for a moment and just imagine the eternal rest where we don't have to worry any more, a place of pure goodness and no evil thoughts to harm one another. This is what I love the most? I can live it now, right now while in this flesh body where wearing that is only temporary. As long as we are faithful and loyal to the end we can live forever and more in peace. While on earth we must continue to struggle towards the mark with pain by our side. In the end there is greater reward only to the faithful and loyal ones to me who are determined to live again in peace.

Lefty says: I have also learned while in this body is that pain releases from the frame a love language, her-emotions are known and has been demonstrating her spirit to all the world.

Lefty says: Pain is pain and will never change. You can try to run and hide but you'll only make things worse on yourselves, or let me say you that is in me will make it harder and push us further into the night or the darkness.

Lefty says: Pain has weight me down to the point this head on these shoulders couldn't take it anymore, I believe that was a moment I felt like I was carrying pounds and pounds of bricks under hot scorching one hundred degree sun with humidity.

Right says: You could forget about a cold front!

Lefty says: As long as pain is avail we can either drown or walk on water.

Lefty says: Souls so what are you going to do?

Lefty says: Pain challenges me to face this material reality; I'm doing some real talking!

Lefty says: I'm must tell you the truth when I say there are times I'm overwhelmed by awful emotions living beside me. There isn't anything I can do except stay cheerful and remain in my place until the storm is over.

Lefty says: I can say it is pain that warns me when troubles are near.

Lefty says Early today this pain had me taken off the stage all because of one thought. What am I to do? I really felt overwhelmed and just plain sick from depression.

Lefty says: This pain is not scripted, this is the real deal and no matter where I go my pain is there ready and willing to intervene, sometimes unexcitingly making me sick-it-tee, sick, sick, sick!

Right says: Influenced you again!

Lefty says: What do you mean you influenced me again?

Right says: Don't play like you didn't know! Look it the words, soulish and poetic, yeah, that's me!

Lefty says: Your pain stabs me repeatedly; there is not anything I can do about this pain who is my neighbor, but I can stand my ground until it's all over.

Lefty says: It's like pain grips this stomach, kidneys, pancreas, and spleen with two hands, digging and twisting at my organs, and on top of that I still stand by my side!

Lefty says: Not understanding this pain I must say is . . . .

Lefty says: I really was tempted to say it, but I had to keep myself under control.

Lefty says: This tongue is dangerous!

Lefty says: You know if we don't get ourselves in alignment with one another it will be our fault.

Lefty says: It is our job to learn how to get along with ourselves before we can get along with other minds outside

Of us who are wearing different tones of skin or even the same colored skin tone.

Lefty says: The fact of the matter is we are spirit only wearing these coats of flesh to get around in this natural world. Every man and women has soul.

Right says: You here that? So don't ever degrade me! Because of my gender, race and the color of my skin, I'm soul now and will always be soul even when this earthly vehicle departs going back to the soils.

Lefty says: My spirit is real and journey's on to a better place, staying positive and remaining faithful has no law only love and joy maintains the real spiritual order keeping peace, unmoved with no pain avail.

Right says: As long as we are here pain will be present and not every soul or spirit has found my ways and because of that these souls are feeling my pain.

Right says: For those who curse me my pain is always avail for them, my pain will be lord and savior over them, read the scripts it says, "There was a certain rich man who was splendidly clothed and who lived each day in luxury. At his door lay a diseased beggar named Lazarus. As Lazarus lay there <u>longing for scraps</u> from the rich man's table, <u>the dogs would come and lick his open sores.</u> Finally, the beggar died and was carried by the angels to be with Abraham. The rich man also died and was buried, and his soul went to the place of the (The spiritual living dead with the same state of mind as he lived in the natural world) dead. There, in torment, he saw Lazarus in the far distance with Abraham.

"The rich man shouted, Father Abraham, have some pity!

Send Lazarus over here to dip the tip of his finger in water and cool my tongue, because I am in anguish in these flames.'

'But Abraham said to him, <u>'Son, remember</u> that during your lifetime you had everything you wanted, and Lazarus had nothing. So now he is here being comforted, and you are in anguish. "Then the rich man said, 'Please, Father Abraham, send him to my father's home. For I have five brothers, and I want him to warn them about this place of torment <u>so they won't have to come here when they die.</u>

'But Abraham said, "Moses and <u>the prophets have warned them.</u> Your

<u>Brothers can read their writings (Because of free will) anytime they want too.</u>'

"The rich man replied, 'No, Father Abraham! But if someone is sent to them from the (spiritual living dead) dead, then they will turn from their sins'

"But Abraham said, 'If they won't listen to Moses and the prophets, they won't listen even if someone rises from the dead.'" Luke 16:19:25-31 NLT.

Lefty says: The rich man had his chance to come to his senses; instead he has chosen not to recognize that one day he will have to die and leave all his possessions behind. The only thing he could think of was that mansion, that car, that money, and that million dollar suite. His thinking I call it is surface thinking, surface thinking is when you only think of the things that has no root to them such these material things of this world that last for a little while then goes back to the earth soils. I must say everything we do with these senses and emotions do effect our real self's that is spiritual, but if we do not recognize that we are spiritual beings only wearing flesh. We will send ourselves to a lost world after this world. The pain the rich man had failed to recognize while above the soils is now attacking him for what he had missed while walking the soils, we are talking for real.

Lefty says: I've learned that having a silver spoon can be a nightmare spiritually; physically there are no struggles only parties, loose hearts and souls with no attachment to the dirt, soul, and mother of us all.

Lefty says: There are a few, who will throw the silver spoon down and find their place of rest, but I must say it is very hard; the road that is narrow is just that narrow. It will be hard for the rich to enter the world of peace, the distractions are great, but at the end of the story there is hope for all and in all there is hope. Rich and poor all have a shot at peace. Amen.

Lefty says: He knew that his emotional side was triggered and crying out to this soul in need, but he suppressed and denied his first love. All this time he had to make amends while living and breathing on the soils. Instead he chooses to remain a stiff-neck with his nose in the air. How hard is it to give someone food at your own table if you are financially rich and could easily buy a restaurant if you want too, I mean how foolish it is to lose your own soul and send your precious creativity and joy to a hell! He is the one who created all this because of his self-centeredness, greed, distorted pride, and just plain ignorance. Hell didn't claim him; he chose to go straight to hell because he let this natural world take complete control over his <u>common sense.</u> How sad it is to see abilities go to waste because of ignorance of one's self. It doesn't take much to give a lending hand, all it takes is just a pinch of letting self-go and God will do the rest. He made his own soul hard and difficult for no reason at all bringing internal torment on himself while he was still walking the soils of earth, and so he will reap what he has sown. What the poor man longed to have and didn't receive while in the natural world. He will receive spiritually; it will be the rich man's turn spiritually to receive the poor man's state of mind of longing for food and water. This time he won't die, this time he's going to be longing for a long time. He's receiving a long sentence at don't want, no not me!

Lefty says: Even the dogs had sense enough to come to the sick man's aid. These dogs didn't reason to themselves and suppress emotions, No! These dogs went with their first instinct and because of this these dogs will be rewarded. After all he had done he still didn't find his humility even in his real spiritual self he didn't recognize his fault, instead he wanted to be the one to come from the dead and tell his brothers and family about his state of mind that is in pain and anguish. These words he has spoken to Abraham should have brought him to his senses, but he has chosen while on earth to become his own worst enemy so now pain attacks him and he must face his own pain that he had denied and suppressed while walking and breathing on the soils of earth.

Lefty says: This natural world is a school for us to recognize that we all must work first in harmony internally, second we must work together in harmony to make a better and safer outer world bringing the kingdom of heaven on earth.

Lefty says: <u>A part of me remembers,</u> this is straight from the author's personal life<u>. I must say that pictures of my mother caring for this woman who was beaten up and robbed it was so amazing to see how my mother came to her aid and help see about her in our apartment house at that time. My mother cleaned her up from her wounds and bandage her, oh yes. My mother has been and still has in her heart a heart for people, thank God that I myself have a heart as well like my mama. It was just surprising to see how my mother spirit took hold and cared for that women. I personally stood there in awe because I have never seen that swift action and instinct, I believe I was about seven or eight years old at the time. Yeah.</u>

Lefty says: Pain had me running away for me that led negativity to consume me.

Right says: You didn't have a clue fear was knocking you down and out!

Right says: My ways had the whole frame trembling, hiding from reality!

Right says: You know, because of my pain and you not recognizing my ways. What a warped mind you had!

Right says: You were soul confused!

Right says: You were soul disturbed that you could've played in the Exorcist!

Right says: Everywhere you look there's pain. And where there's pain my energy is present.

Right says: Who's controlling the left foot, arm, shoulder, left facial express, and eye? ME!

Right says: Keep showing off! All you doing is showing that you haven't known your left hand (Emotions) from your right, Man!

Right says: You reading these words can help, but it's not official if I'm not applied, for real!

Lefty says: There has been a struggle, a quiet struggle not really severe or earth shaking, but it's been a small test to see how I will come out of it. It just helps me to be stronger and more aware of the negative energies intending to overwhelm my joy if I give in to a part of me that is full of fear, anger, and sensual.

Lefty says: Today I am happy and in my place forever and more.

Lefty says: You really think your education is going to save your soul? I must tell me that am in you is that you must first know my place and then your character and your personality will be salt to the world as well as your education, pain will not be your problem but will be your source to create beautiful music to Heal, Relate, Capture, Transform, Enlighten, And bring insight into a lost and confused world filled with false images, stereotypes, and a lack of understanding.

Lefty says: Pain is just piercing my house intending to take my joy deeper into the places that isn't happy, but through all this I am still. This pain will not turn me into a victim but a champion who was said that he will never mound to anything!

Right says: You said in the scripts, 'Do not be afraid, my people!

You know that from ancient times until now I have predicted all that would happen, and you are my witnesses. ISAIAH 44:8 GNT.

Right says: 'But let me tell you something!

You know I'm the one who's creativity, insight, emotional, seeing the whole picture, and surely I'm the one possessing dreams, visions, prophecies and predictions!

Right says: You said yourself! Man does not eat bread alone!

Right says: You're just the writer and spokesman! Leave the creativity and insight to me!

Right says: Now as long as we in harmony and in agreement, isn't the God of the universe present?

Lefty says: Yes. This day I am not alone together we unite showing the world God is in action.

Lefty says: If pain takes over me the tongue and mouth remains shy, timid and mute.

Right says: If you give me one inch! I'm consuming! That's all it takes one scary movie.

Lefty says: Look, I am not a problem as long as I'm in my place, Joy is mine! And I will not be a problem but the solution to the problem.

Right says: Feeling my pain isn't bad if I'm in my place.

Lefty says: I'm not living in the past today I happy that I can move forward, but history will always exist. Where there is history there is pain, where there is pain there is history.

Lefty says: Pain is a part of me only to show that I myself am not alone on this journey while driving this flesh vehicle made of dirt and soil.

Lefty says: My image is not pain, but again I must say that pain walks with me giving us the soul to get through the valleys of death.

Lefty says: I must say without pain I couldn't make it through the wilderness un-harmed.

Right says: You know! Without a doubt! That you would not be speaking, reading, writing, and using that mouth to prophesy!

Right says: You know! You wouldn't be using words like remembering and words like pain and anguish! You better recognize! I'm that movie you keep playing in that head of yours, yeah that's me! I'm the one you using every time you prophesy and say predictions! You see me now!

Recognize my place you readers of this word!

Right says: Didn't the scripts say, 'Remember that you are my servant.' ISAIAH 44:21 GNT.

Lefty says: I must say it was pain that saved my soul from a cell, and I'm not talking about this natural world prison, NO! I'm talking somewhere billions reside right now as I speak. A place where there are billions of ME's who are just like me. Where is my joy? My joy here is consumed by my wild and screaming emotions that I let rule over me while on the soils walking and breathing.

Lefty says: To those who are living and breathing on top the soils, take heed my joy is never unfailing to those who recognize that I am the spokesman in all, I am your host when things are painful, bad and when things are good.

Lefty says: If pain is a part of me who shall I fear, natural bodies die and turn back to dirt and soil, but my emotions remain intact forever and ever, so who shall I fear? Fear Is fear so If I give up and hand my joy over to fear I'm creating my own prison cell not only for me but for me who believes in me that is in them. So I tell me out there that it is not the financial riches that are going to save your soul. It is the pain and anguish that is leading the soul to brokenness, turning my ways into humility and love.

Lefty says: No man is powerful without love.

Right says: You right about that!

Lefty says: With love by my side I'm not worried; the attackers have become their own worst enemy by drowning themselves with fear.

Lefty says: The spiritual applies to us first, because we are spirit energies wearing this coat of flesh. Knowing my place is all I need to know. Joy is already in my possession; truly I am happy to be able to tap into my place of good cheer. The best part about knowing my place is that there is no law in this natural world that can stop my joy from being expressed. The law I possess is spirit, and as long as I am in harmony with my first love. There is not anything on this earth that can separate me from me, and when we are in agreement surely the spirit of God is present.

Lefty says: As long as there is pain there will be creativity and insight avail."

THE GENTLENESS IS A PART OF ME & THE AUTHORS PERSONALITY

BOOK TWO, CHAPTER NINE

THE GENTLENESS IS A PART OF ME

Lefty says: "I must say that I have a choice to either accept the measure of gentleness that is a part of me or I can rebel and become my own problem and walking nightmare, yeah, while still walking these soils.

2. Lefty says: You know what though? I'd rather accept me than to live in confusion and at war with me.

3. Lefty says: There is no handouts you either get to know gentleness or be on the run fleeing from me as long as I'm living and breathing up on the soils.

4. Right says: Isn't it my ways that gives the body rhythm, grace and soul?

5. Lefty says: Gentleness is us when we harmonize. This is obedience to the spiritual law.

6. Lefty says: Meek and lowliness.

7. Right says: That's ME!

8. Lefty says: I have been a witness and now I must admit that gentleness has been distorted and used for erroneous deeds.

9. Lefty says: I myself have fallen once upon a time a few seasons ago and when I say that it hurts, it hurts when your worse night mares are reality.

10. Lefty says: Please listen! I am not asking any man to forgive my sins, but I myself personally must leave this natural world one day and face me, but when I do leave I can know that I did not leave this natural state with hate and resentment in my heart and mind.

11. Lefty says: She is gentleness that has been talked about for centuries and admired throughout pictures, written literature, ancient poetry's, songs, dancing and most of all history.

12. Lefty says: Gentleness is my help when times get very unhappy. The gentle one is there to keep me from displacement and from being over happy.

13. Lefty says: To sum it all up I must say that if I do not distinguish my character from the gentle one that is a part of me I will surely become emotionally disturbed leading myself on to harm's path way. And when I say this is not good, this is not good, I'm talking honest whether I'm accepted or not I know I'm a be ok.

    Right says: You want more?

14. Lefty says: This gentleness that is a part of me has been mingling with identities that are not good. The truth is these identities are colder than zero degrees, calculating, and leaving no room to breathe and rest.

15. Lefty says: Gentleness gives me relief and ease when I am thinking too much with reasoning I'm possessing every day you look at me in the mirror you readers and lovers of this word of inspiration.

16. Lefty says: I've learned that there are some words that are hard to express gentleness, because

gentleness is spoken through actions, words only secondary.

17. Lefty says: Poetic books speak about her charm and her persuasiveness, gentleness; all of us reading these words possess gentleness whether you accept or reject.

18. Right says: For real we aren't playing!

19. Right says: Charming the whole world brothers and sis.

20. Right says: We all up and around in the bible!

21. Right says: You can easily find me if you really want to know me!

22. Right says: I'm not that hard to find!

23. Right says: You say you love me souls do something about it! Stop being Lazy!

24. Right says: I'm not holding anything back, you holding me back from my full expressions, for real!

25. Right says: My love is known, so what cha going to do? Flee like a coward and live in rocks and caves! It's your choice my brothers and sisters.

26. Right says: To all of you who desire my insight you better get right!

27. Right says: You sure won't have a problem finding peace if you reading about me this very moment, we real genuine and my emotions of fire! You feel my spirit? This spirit real!

28. Right says: Keep on desiring me! Soon, very soon! You will find me!

29. Right says: Find me a place, a sacred quiet place to pray and meditate! It's not that hard to be alone to pray with me!

30. Right says: You want everything but you don't even seek me!

31. Right says: We rather play cards all day and gossip about junk mail!

    Right says: You know you love to talk!

32. Lefty says: I am happy this very moment knowing gentleness is right beside me.

Right says: Don't be giving me these happy looks! I'm seeing joy out there in the world is caught up in some mess all the time because of fear, anger, hate, and confusion.

33. Right says: All of this plays out on stage because of ignorance and lack of knowledge of joy and me, for real!

34. Right says: Amen somebody!

35. Right says: I'm crying all the time!

36. Right says: Look for me and you can find my love that is in you. It's real now!

Lefty says: I must say to all of you that are in me out there Are we truly, I mean are we really hungry for peace? Ask me that am in you that question. <u>I'm being for real!</u>

37. Right says: You see how my emotional ways played a role?

Lefty says: Aren't we getting off the subject?

Right says: Off the subject! Boy!

Right says: If it weren't for meekness created by meekness there is no subject! Brother!

Lefty says: You right! Together we bring images and subjects to the table to help ourselves in the billions. When we harmonize there is perfect understanding of Gods universe.

38. Right says: Peace of mind is our pursuit for all of ME's soul sick-lee.

   Right says: If you seek you can find my warmth that is in me, who am you, silly.

   Right says: I'm soul kindness, gentleness, lowliness, even Jesus said, Take my yoke upon you, (That is you) and Iearn of me; <u>for I am meek and lowly in heart: and ye shall find rest unto your souls.</u> Matt 11:29 KJV.

   <u>Right says:</u> Are you serious bro! You know that I alone can do but so much alone?

   Lefty says: Remember that I am the spokesman for you and I; I am the spirit man holding good cheer in my possession when it seems there is no lifting of our heavy burdens, I am the one who releases stress from the facial and body express.

Right says: OK. Now tell me how you release this stress?

Lefty says: First, You should know that joy is in me. Second, I want you to take a pen or a pencil and a piece of writing paper it doesn't matter what type of paper as long as the pen and pencil can write on the paper. Third, I want me that am you to write with the right hand that I'm controlling for about two minutes. After you have done the steps I want you to switch hands and use left hand, but if you are a left hander use the right hand next. Right handers should feel by using the left hand a soothing. For you left handers using the right hand an uplifted or outstanding feeling.

Lefty says: Even Jesus said in the scriptures, '<u>But when thou doest alms, let not thy left hand (Emotions) know what thy right hand (Emotions) doeth.</u>' Matt 6:3 KJV.

Right says: Wow! I'm just shock.

Right says: You really think these folks reading bibles, or even have a bible? Are you kidding me!

Lefty says: All we have to do is just study this book of me and study the bible to show ourselves we are approved and worthy to face me.

39. Right says: You readers really for sure are now going to feel me! Read on! Read that Book of ME and The Bible! Tapping into me shouldn't be an issue now!

Right says: I'm for real! We aren't playing

Brothers and sisters!

Right says: Playing in the sand box is over!

Lefty says: Now if you readers are right handed and have not done what I have written or not interested in your own functions. You have no time to see and feel what is in you. You show me even if the dead were to rise from the spiritual world you still wouldn't believe in me.

Right says: You readers know you denying me as well?

Right says: I'm so down to earth, but you still acting a fool!

Right says: I'm telling you now that if you reading other literature from now on you'll see that I'm in all spitting insight. I'm not going anywhere, soul you might as well get with the program and accept this gentleness.

40. Lefty says: Hold on just a little longer. I am with me; don't give up because you're too close to the finish line brothers and sisters. I am with me always no matter what is happening in all of our lives.

Authors Personality

Right says: Who is jaysoula? That's me.

Lefty says: I kind of like that name. Jaysoula is soul beautiful and lovely, who is a part of me now, tomorrow, and forever and more Amen.

Lefty says: You know as a man and with you by my side. I have just fallen in love with you and that name. I know we said we wouldn't give a name a way, but your charm is irresistible and unpredictable.

Lefty says: <u>My helper always recognizes the need</u> and so that let me know without my helper I'm just as cold as ice or let me say I'll be turning into cold hate.

Lefty says: You are my first love and I can never deny nor reject my first love, because without you my helper I am not whole. You are a part of me whether I deny you or intend to ignore. This day I have chosen to walk with me in harmony and in oneness.

Lefty says: I can love me."

LET IT FLY (POETRY ONE, MONEY, & MORE INSIGHT

BOOK THREE, CHAPTER TEN

POETRY ONE

Right says: "You can dish it out but you can even stay in the heat! And you say you know me.

2.   Right says: Your state of mind is still the same, you let fear that am in me that is also in you take you down and not up. You have chosen hell and rejoice in it.

3.   Right says: You use me just like you used up your physical relationships.

4.   Right says: You condemn me and then have the nerve to use me for your personal pleasures.

5.   Right says: How dare you mislead, sending mixed signals to the world!

6.   Right says: Man isn't learning like he ought to learn, because he's distracted by women, money, and the things of this natural world.

7.   Right says: You anger me! You choose to suppress and send everything you can to hell with me that am in you.

8.   Right says: My anger is not out of control, but if you don't know what is mine there is no way anger is under control, you're out of control consumed by negativity, devilish characteristics, If you're reading souls, Get a grip and know my emotions isn't dead, my spirit is alive and active, for real!

9.   Right says: You need to learn my patience, but you alone it's like trying to train a lion by yourself in the wild with no instructions, I'm for real! Amen!

10.   Right says: Don't get all religious on me just because I'm saying Amen!

11.   Right says: That's what's wrong with me that am in you now! Jesus spoke about you folks in the bible, but you still use me for money sending out mixed signals.

12. Right says: You have already denied womanish emotions and then you claim you're the man. You aren't anything without me! Let me just get that in your left brains, Man!

13. Right says: Everyone wants knowledge and still denies me when knowledge is found!

14. Lefty says: Why is this? Because fear hasn't been understood, that's why roots are uprooted from the soil by title waves. Fear, out of control anger, and hate have become there lord and savior.

15. Right says: You really think your knowledge is going to save you? I'm going tell you like it is that if you don't know my place, what a scary night mare.

16. Right says: You want basics! Read about me!

    You want basics! Study me!

    You want basics! Know what is in me!

    You want basics! Recognize that I'm lowly!

17. Right says: You say you want to look for me, I'm right here!

18. Right says: What's all the fuss about?

19. Right says: Loving me means you are all the way free, and inside there isn't any debates here!

20. Right says: Keep on running from me, I'm a get me that is in you readers one day. You must forget that I'm beneath that head of yours materially, but spiritually I'm always present whether you accept me or not.

21. Right says: Soul what's up now!

22. Right says: When you readers do find my love don't let me out there in the world mislead me that am you, you understand what I'm saying brothers and sis?

23. Right says: Isn't my language graceful and beautiful?

24. Right says: My emotional ways can raise me that am in you into a place of high positions, authority, power, and leadership.

25. Right says: Obeying my gentleness leads to greatness.

26. Right says: For you who claim leadership but have chosen to not express my spiritual language through this body made of flesh you will go into your own cell that is not seen with the natural eye, so if you deny her that is me you will be cut down from power there's no doubt about that, read Deuteronomy twenty eight we isn't playing!

27. Right says: No man is man alone without his helper, feel my emotions?

28. Lefty says: You have made men so afraid to face you, but all this is for the spiritual growth, so fear and all the negative feelings can be under your control.

29. Right says: We all desire and want what we already have, for real! Now if you reading about me that is you know I'm right.

30. Right says: You readers need some life assurance, and no not life insurance. As long as you have breath and are conscious and walking these soils there is still hope.

31. Right says: You out there who deny your children you deny yourself and will pay for your sins, for real! Think I'm playing! Amen!

32. Right says: I'm feeling suppressed! You know what though your only fueling me to spew my peace even harder, creativity sizzles wearing soils call me Ms. Riddles sending movies to hero's, seeking more hungry then leno's my soul more realer than this, world is sicker loves liquor, where there's soul this face summits, see love? You're sick! Vomit.

33. Lefty says: Why are you angry?

34. Right says: If these spirits keep tip tapping, we spitting more words, we shocking the world, isn't soul sick, I'm tired of this bull!

35. Right says: Bench sitters never get know playing time, soul what now throw it all away? For those hungry families out there you eaten I'm making sure of that!

36. Right say: You out there claim you faced me, but don't even know your left hand from your right, and if you don't know the basics how in the world you going claim your hard son and daughters, brothers and sisters, common sense says if you don't know your right hand emotions from your left you in trouble! For real! I'm saying this not to scare me. I'm being real genuine with me because I'm a love me regardless, no matter what my conditions are at this time!

37.   Right says: You Rappers, Singers, jazz, musicians, Dancers, all of you out there you tap into me twenty four seven, seven days a week, 365 days out the year, souls don't tell me you didn't find me! Now let me hear you say it? That's real talk!

38.   Right says: I'm not the happy go lucky type.

39.   Right says: I'm like the croc laying low in the earthly swamps leaving the analyzing to reason on the left hand side of me, you feeling my spirit?

40.   Right says: I'm a say this! If my fear is not in place! You know what kind of mind you'll have? Zzzzzzzzzzzzzzzzzzzzzzzzzzzz.

41.   Right says: Yeah! I'm not playing!

42.   Right says: I'm for real and genuine!

MONEY

Right says: You love money so much, but money isn't the problem!

2. Lefty says: I have given you money for your every need. It is the choices we make that bring unnecessary harm and pain into our intestines, stomach, heart, and mind, for real.

3. Lefty says: Money isn't the problem it is how we handle and manage it.

4. Lefty says: Going into debt is our choice. What we want and what we need all come down to us making a decision to go into debt or avoid debt.

The choice is ours. No one can make that decision for us. If I want to go to college it takes money. I can either go into debt or avoid it.

5.   Lefty says: If I want a house I can either go into debt or avoid it. It's that simple!

6.   Lefty says: You have a choice to save your money to pay off your debt.

7.   Lefty says: No one can make that decision for you. You must make that decision because you are in control of your destiny.

8.   Lefty says: You control your own fate.

9.   Lefty says: You can use money for anything you want if you have enough of it to get what you want and need.

10.   Lefty says: The point I'm saying is I must maintain my self-control if I want to see an empire, money plays a major role meaning if I'm not connected to my help, my spirit counselor. I'm throwing hard earned money away man!

11.   Lefty says: The word money stimulates the mind getting every soul excited.

12. Right says: Those souls are saying, I'm a get mine! Money strikes a fire inside and it doesn't take much for my mind to be on high alert naturally. Money should be distributed equally from the poor, middle class, and the rich, but for them who earned their riches legally and honestly these folks no matter what class, it is fair to say that creativity stands out and deserves the name peculiar. Illegally, spiritually you are selling your soul out for that money high.

13. Right says: You know why minds are called by us money high?

14. Right says: This money high is when no mind out there can tell you anything! A couple bucks just consumed his head and heart.

15. Right says: When it's all said and done where is he or she?

16. Right says: What looks good isn't always good to buy with the money brothers and sisters.

17. Right says: Either Physically decaying in the soils, rehab, prison, or walking the streets sickly in soul, heart, and mind. Even the scripts say, 'Then (Jealousy, hate, greed, and negative energy consumed him.) Satan entered into Judas, called

Iscariot, who was one of the twelve disciples. So Judas went off and spoke with the chief priests and the officers of the Temple guard about how he could betray Jesus to them. They were pleased and <u>offered to pay him money.</u> <u>Judas agreed to it</u> and started looking for a good chance to hand Jesus over to them without the people knowing about it. Luke 22:3-6 GNT.

18. Right says: You see what happens when you aren't right! You get money high!

19. Lefty says: May we all learn from our mistakes and not let our money highs get the best of us.

20. Right says: Keep being misled and puffed up in your money highs! You'll see me! Look at all your Judases throughout history and in your history today, still betraying me for money!

21. Right says: I'm a show you what money highs will do for my soul. Money doesn't always bring happy endings, so stay alert and aware at all times, for real. Money used for wrong purposes can definitely have its consequences, don't believe take a look at Judas end, scripts say, 'When Judas, the traitor, learned that Jesus had been condemned, he repented and took back the (Money) thirty silver coins to the chief priests and the elders. "I have

sinned by betraying an innocent man to death!" he said.

"What do we care about that?" they answered. "<u>That is your business!</u>" Judas threw the coins down in the Temple and left; then he went off and hanged himself. Matt 27:3-5 GNT.

22.   Right says: You see what happens when I'm not recognized? He let my fear overcome him!

23.   Right says: Money was not the problem, he let it his own high and greed blind him, thinking he would benefit by turning Jesus in, but little did he realize that it would back fire on him, and it did!

24.   Right says: My emotions overwhelmed and defeated him. His actions had no reason only self—hate, guilt, fear, sorrow, all the negative emotions over took him because he didn't recognize that hope was still avail for him, but instead he quickly without a doubt ended his life. Money only triggers a high that comes from us not the money you see and feel what I'm saying? No doubt about that brothers and sisters.

25.   Lefty says: Don't sell your soul for money, because at the end of the day I must face the consequences of my own actions.

26. Lefty says: I'm must say that if I am not in place fear and hate can definitely take advantage of the opportunity. So don't be a victim, stay alert and aware of me that am you."

MORE INSIGHT

Lefty says: I've said that when I'm overwhelmed by you it's like I become mute, no words are coming out this mouth.

2. Right says: I'm the one remembering past events; you must forget the only way you can feel and imagine is through me, feel me my spirit now? I'm letting all of me that is also in you read about me, though I'm not the reader only the magician spreading inspirational spirit energies from out of you to the next inspired, even Moses was inspired sending shock waves throughout generations, amazing isn't how we all have the same eye?

3. Right says: Lose your courage gloom and doom as all over them cheerful facials, for real!

4. Right says: Folks if you watching tell-a-vision, take notes! And don't eat up the kitchen! Feel what I'm saying!

5. Right says: Learn some survival skills for once in your life! Amen!

6. Right says: Don't neglect your house, clean up!

7. Lefty says: Learn from mistakes and turn problems into solutions, not every soul can or will accept me for me, but I must remain with me to the end, because when I leave this material world I will leave alone and will be buried alone if there is a burial, see me now?

8. Lefty says: I came into this world physically alone and I will depart physically alone whether I am taking alive by higher energies or remain decaying in the earth physically.

   Lefty says: Whatever I do with me I am held responsible, but if it is coming from other's it is not my responsibility. Every soul is responsible for his or her destination in the world of spirit.

9.   Lefty says: Some time I'm talking Just talking negative, all because you interfering with me.

10. Right says: Well if you stay in place you wouldn't be your enemy!

11. Lefty says: I know fear is not mine, my place is secure.

12. Lefty says: Discipline is not mines alone, you and I are workers to help this body work in agreement, talking for real.

13. Right says: I'm showing my secrets all the time and you reading always missing it!

14. Right says: I'm not your enemy unless you continue denying my ways, I'm telling you we aren't playing!

15. Lefty says: Any time you brush your teeth or look in the mirror, just remember I am that cheerful Joyous smile on that face, anger isn't mine if you want to know the truth.

16. Right says: I'm tired of all of you story tellers! And I'm not talking novels and fiction stories out a book! You know what we saying!

17. Right says: Now if you want me, you must come honestly laying your wrongs down before me if you want to accept me who is beautiful, graceful, inspirational, poetic, soul is me, so if you want my love you must submit.

18. Right says: If man wants to succeed and live he must recognize my emotions or else he's doomed, revelations, we aren't playing!

19. Right says: He really wants to try and buy me things, he forgetting all I'm asking for is that he recognizes me that am a part him, for real!

20. Right says: If I'm in my place he is always seeking my love!

21. Right says: All I'm asking is if he submits to me, I'm show my insights and reveal my knowledge, but if I'm not in order you is a doomed man! Simple as that! Let the Book of Revelations and the seals come open!

Right says: Come and see!

Right says: We are acting soul crazy!

Right says: We are soul backwards it's unheard of; we not even close to being equally yoked, dividing and hiding from ourselves! Where's my simplicity!

22. Right says: You know if he is in his place and we in agreement! There is not anything on earth or under the earth messing with us!

   Right says: I'm for real!

23. Right says: It's time to come back to me! You better find me, because mercy leaving soon!

24. Lefty says: What women do it's my half expression.

25. Lefty says: Without my half theirs is no sweet cakes.

26. Lefty says: I have found my place knowing joy is on this face I'm controlling. Together in harmony always with no doubt that sweet cake is by my side, now, tomorrow, and like the bible says forever and more.

27. Right says: If we want to be polite and courteous Just know I'm right there beside you calling out to you saying, I'm here! I'm here! Stop running from me! I'm here to help you! Stop!

28. Right says: You want love love is just that—Love!

29. Lefty says: Who is responsible for love?

30. Right says: Who is responsible! You and I!

31. Right says: Man really needs me or else he's giving both of us a one way ticket to an unseen prison! Even as we live on the soils.

32. Right says: I'm not about get myself caught up in some mess! I'm in my place! I'm staying right here!

33. Lefty says: There is so many out there just like us getting caught up in some dangerous woods.

34. Right says: Woods! You aren't talking tiger are you?

35. Lefty says: NO. The wilderness is attracting millions and still fear is knocking us around, melting us down, and Making us into cheerless beggars.

36. Lefty says: If I cannot commune with me that is her I'm not in place, fury burns me and is ready to surface like an active volcano ready to erupt the surface.

37. Lefty says: When there is no communion their inner conflict.

38. Lefty says: When we are in communion and in our place, this love is richer than all the money in the world.

39. Lefty says: Surely a part me must have her freedom, this is a spiritual law but at the end of the day her submission is with her—man and man to her-woman.

40. Lefty says: A man must trust his women, women must trust her man, intuition and insight or a feeling of suspicion can bring negativity to the surface, so the best way to Face self is to come in gentleness not in insecurity, jealousy, hate, and anger but in love to your help mate, without condemnation and resentment.

41. Lefty says: Your emotional control keeps the peace, keeping the heart from being troubled.

42. Lefty says: Don't trouble yourselves to destruction it only takes a word that can lead to the wrong actions.

43. Lefty says: It's good that one can endure the pain when he or she is corrected, but I'm telling all of

me out there that it is even better to remain in your place when the pain is brand new, how many can endure pain and remain sound?

44. Right says: I'm not about to disown my place! I'm going to be fine!

45. Right says: All I'm saying is if you recognize,

    Finding me you find that faith you have been looking for!

46. Right says: You deny me you deny my abilities, insight that is in you is useless and you're still a problem!

47. Lefty says: Fear is not mine, Joy is mine.

    Right says: You know what the problem with man today? He's been controlled by his own fear and what the world would say about him.

48. Lefty says: If it weren't for imaginations there wouldn't be any creativity and the world as we know it today wouldn't be in existence.

49. Lefty says: I am the spokesman, without creativity there is no creator.

50. Lefty says: The spokesman is the host while the creator, the artist designs oneself.

51. Lefty says: What a part of me records my creation records.

52. Right says: I'm the one holding music and all of them lyrics!

53. Right says: You just speak what I'm giving you, I'm helping you!

54. Right says: How many times I'm a have mercy on you who act like you can get away with your (Ignorance) evil? I'm sick and tired!

55. Right says: My mercy cannot fail!

56. Right says: You who take advantage and keep hurting my feelings I'm sending your bodies back to the soil!

57. Right says: You have shown me that you only have cares for this world; this world will be your state of mind forever and more!

58. Right says: You have chosen me only to follow your ugliness; you hurt me to please your flesh!

59. Right says: What you have done will be done to you in the next life!

60. Right says: For those who willingly capture and embrace my ways have learned to face me, the mirror is not a problem no more to them!

61. Right says: I'm already knowing how I'm thinking, so souls who you think you trying to fool? I'm on top of the way you thinking!

62. Lefty says: Jealousy wants me but I am not giving my joy up for negativity. It is better for me to remain in my place then to give in to negative energies living next to me.

63. Lefty says: Let me say this, man is not a man if weakness is avail. Without weakness there is no defending and when there is no defending there is no protecting!

    Lefty says: There wouldn't even be love, soul, affection, the world as we know it would be cold.

    Right says: Zero below!

64. Right says: Heart isn't like wax now, now is it?

65. Right says: As long as I'm living with me, you will always be on my list, escaping!

    Right says: You aren't going anywhere!

    You really think when you leave this natural state you free from me? Wrong again!

66. Right says: I'm not your enemy unless you choose to deny my ways!

67. Lefty says: My mind, my sphere has in the past have been consumed by fear and hate, but this day I am wearing my joyful expressions proudly without doubt mingling in my house.

68. Lefty says: Most of the time I do come on very strong, but in the end it's to benefit all of my cheerful facials wearing all colors of skin, talking for real genuine.

69. Lefty says: If I live my life for my own greed and without love helping me. I am already living the worst parts of the book of revelations.

70. Lefty says: When I'm moving the heart without a doubt is going to relief stress.

71. Lefty says: I am meek only when I am in harmony with my helper, my counselor, my teacher, my weakness.

72. Right says: Don't be afraid of me! Don't let man's words he's written control and suppress me by using my fear to control the world! Face me with all your strength no matter what this god of this world has done to you!

73. Right says: As long as we are in communion I'm not my enemy, but if you reading do deny my emotional hand you setting your own self up to fall!

    Right says: You readers know what happens when I'm out of pocket with me?

    Right says: I'm attacked by my own fear and hate!

    Right says: You know what else is happening to me?

    Right says: I'm fully possessing them joyful facials, man is now really possessed!

74. Right says: He is no gentle man now! He is a beast man!

75. Lefty says: I am now like an animal consumed by reptilian characteristics sort of like a mean crocodile laying low in the lake for hours awaiting for them impalas to dip their heads over for a drink of water in the lake.

    Lefty says: I don't just speak to me this very moment but I am speaking and writing to all of me who don't even recognize the animal within is alive and willing to consume you readers, so be aware and alert at all times for the <u>devilish sphere</u> living within and waiting for us to lose balance and harmony within.

76. Lefty says: If I and meekness who is my helper loses connection. I am in conflict giving my neighbor the chance to war against me.

77. Right says: My Job is to use my creativity while a part of me remains joyful and glad!

78. Right says: When it's all said and done we are together now and forever and more!

    Right says: You like that!

    Right says: Let me say this! Happy and meek is in their place, but who can understand and walk the walk?

79. Right says: We must admit though, without me there is no new song!

80. Lefty says: It's about that time for me to take heed to the way I function. I am talking honestly to me that am also in you readers.

81. Lefty says: I can't even speak when fear seated beside me causes me to look drunk when I don't even drink.

    Right says: You do drink!

    Lefty says: What alcohol do we drink?

    Right says: Not alcohol but juices and milk!

    Lefty says: Very funny.

    Right says: We all drink! It doesn't have to be alcohol just because of the word we use such as drinkers!

    Right says: You can drink yourselves to death though on anything far that goes, you feeling my ways and insights right about now?

82. Lefty says: Don't send my joy to the lower mind state after this natural body is deceased that we

are controlling brothers and sisters. Why? Because precious am I who is in this universe living in all, even in you who is reading about me.

Right says: I'm really furious with me right about now! I'm angry with me!

Right says: You out siders back off me! Only me out there that am in all has experienced and knows what I'm saying!

83.   Right says: How long must we deal with these sick ME's who don't want me to help them to stand with meek?

84.   Lefty says: This world is not my problem nor is the things in it. I have chosen to walk and not look back at past disorders in the mind.

85.   Lefty says: The greatest teacher has a helper.

Right says: ME!

86.   Lefty says: Let me say this that if I lose myself from being overwhelmed by fear and anger. I am already slipping down the broad path of wild and uncontrollable emotions, I don't want that part of me to rule over me like it did Cain, he killed his brother because of his jealousy and rage, if you

don't know read about it isn't going anywhere, all in the scriptures.

87. Right says: I'm not so bad once you get to know my emotions make up your true identity, soul now what!

   Right says: What cha going to say now?

   Right says: O. OK. Let's get with me that am you and learn!

   Right says: Some of you reading probably had some smooth path ways, but let me say that if you don't know you want grow!

88. Right says: You want acts of kindness to be genuinely expressed, get to know my beautiful!

89. Right says: Can you sing? Well, if you even attempted you have attempted me!

90. Right says: My emotions aren't a joke!

   Lefty says: I must say that my good cheerful expressions are real as well.

91. Lefty says: I know how I sound when I'm saying; I am the remote controller of this right eye, right hand, right foot, and right toe.

92. Right says: You really mechanical! Mr. I, robot!

93. Right says: Whether you deny me or not, guess what? I'm still in you and with you!

Right says: Even the scriptures describe my devilish characteristics that am in all of you, yes you! You're not exempt! Scripts say," and the donkeys were in a nearby pasture.

Suddenly the Sabeans <u>attacked and stole them all.</u> <u>They killed every one</u> of your servants except me. Before he could finish speaking, another servant came and said, "<u>Lightning struck the sheep and the</u> shepherds and killed them all.

Before he finished speaking, another servant came and said, "<u>Three bands of Chaldean raiders</u> <u>attacked us, took away the camels, and killed all</u> <u>your servants except</u> me. I am the only one who escaped to tell you."

"Your children were having a feast at the home of your oldest son, <u>when a storm swept in from the</u>

desert. <u>It blew the house down and killed them all.</u> Job 1:14-19 GNT.

Right says: Now you see my emotions!

Right says: Now you see my energies!

Right says: You folks always fighting against me, you rather send me straight to . . . . you know where!

Right says: You use me . . . all you! What do you think I'm not worthy to be here with you, you chose me!

94.   Right says: I'm going tell you readers that if my negative ways aren't dealt with and is out of place, harms path you know is near!

Right says: Why do you mess and play with my emotions? I'm not smiling!

Right says: You playing with me!

Right says: All I'm saying to me that am in you is to get right!

95. Lefty says: As long as we are in agreement love I know is possible, there is no confusion only love and joy.

96. Lefty says: Her spirit is real and genuine, but she needs me if she wants to live in harmony.

    Lefty says: If she is not understood the whole frame is shaking, walking in suspense, definitely in fear.

97. Right says: You writing about me all the time through, Magazines, fiction, non-fiction; you the one writing about me I'm just a help mate.

98. Right says: Who's feeling and looking depressed all in face? Me.

    Right says: That's my emotions brothers and sisters.

99. Lefty says: Pain comes first then joy.

100. Lefty says: If my joyful emotions are KO'd by emotions of fear. I'm my own dangerous weapon wearing this coat, flesh we call it.

101. Right says: I'm not trying to prosper!

102. Right says: I'm just sure this place mine!

103. Lefty says: A good honest, understandable speech with common sense can win me over.

104. Lefty says: Why do you, emotional spirit intend to overcome me?

    Right says: Write it down on paper and read it over and over again! Is that hard?

105. Right says: You can't even speak clearly when I'm flooding taking over speech!

106. Right says: You who are reading think you know me, we'll see who's recognizing!

    Lefty says: Hell's fury isn't having my spirit not now, not ever. I am ready to stand by my side, call me kick stand I am sure my joy is rich living in my house.

107. Lefty says: Man and women have chosen to swim in shark infested waters.

    Lefty says: There are times when I'm feeling like this joy that is in me takes away all the worries of this life completely; the next moment I'm on the end of a building fifty stories high ready to dive head first; It doesn't matter your rank, position, background, education, color of skin, because at the end of the story we all are spirits wearing this flesh like long trench coats, seriously.

Right says: Ouch! That hurts.

Lefty says: I encourage all of you reading about me that am in you not to end or shorting your journey, you don't want to have to come back and start all over.

Lefty says: I'm good, that is only when we are working as one. It doesn't matter what emotions I possess. There must be weakness to balance out.

108. Lefty says: If I say I hate those who aren't trying to change, that make me a problem unsolved mystery.

109. Right says: Just know I've been around for centuries, decades, and millenniums, don't believe you need to get right!

110. Right says: Earth is me, earthly and yup! Down to earth!

Right says: Speech no avail here!

Right says: All you (liars) story tellers living in fear of me you will feel my pain!

111. Right says: I'm emotions raging boiling over, center, top, and above the earth, everybody made is fire, we can't even rest because of me, emotional waves trigger mother spirit energies, I'm soul earthly if you don't believe look around.

112. Right says: If my anger is not in place there is no doubt your upturned happy facial express is sickness.

113. Lefty says: As long as I'm with me and in harmony, hell on this earth will not be mine, you reading and deny, it's your choice if you want stay on hell and dance. I'm living soundly with no doubt.

    Lefty says: Why do I have to suffer this long?

    Right says: I'm treating you hard to purge you!

114. Right says: This body is dirt whether we can accept it or not that's the way we were created.

115. Lefty says: I'm not about to hurt myself, pain is not mine but I'm sure my joy is real and can never be completely crushed as long as I am with my first love living in harmony.

116. Right says: Your joy has encouraged billions, remember my movies can be sour and joyful so you reading about yourselves just remember you readers control your own destiny!

117. Right says: It's like every moment we type I'm getting flashes of what is to come or what has already been, seriously!

118. Right says: Admitting to you this day that you have been my spokesman and my protector.

119. Lefty says: My Joy is rich sending waves of encouragement to the whole world.

119. Lefty says: Faces are relieved from stressful days at work because of me; a little laughter heals a broken heart, so let's get some this Joy into the world.

120. Right says: You still need me! You Joy into the world.

121. Lefty says: My house is open to all who is willing to find my face, my good cheer, my confidence.

122. Right says: You wouldn't invite anyone into your house without meekness!

123. Lefty says: This is not the end of the world so it's no need to worry, my positive spirit energy is real and I don't worry about what this devilish world say about me. I am this day with me together we are manifesting the present of God who is light, energy, in all and is a part of all. Amen!"

MY DREAMS & SPIRITUAL EXPERIENCES

BOOK THREE, CHAPTER ELEVEN

Lefty says: "To truly get understanding of your dreams write them down when the dreams are fresh in your own theatre.

2. Right says: Dreams are in me taking front stage when reason is not avail; sleep is my time to show you our worlds; happy and sad worlds, for real!

3. Lefty says: You can dream about whatever you want too, you are given a part of me to decide your worlds.

4. Lefty says: Through my own experience with me who is my neighbor, helper, and counselor is the

one has taken us as a young mind to a horrific place; the catch to it all was I never stopped . . . .

5.   Lefty says: You readers might ask you never stopped what? I never stopped falling and burning; every moment that I was falling I really felt like this was a wakeup call almost like a warning before the storms. Yes at the age of 11, here I am a young mind with dreams like this I didn't understand at the time. The year was 1990.

6.   Lefty says: A part of me remembers the dream in 2001. At that time I was 21 years old. It was a time fear was still causing me to flinch and hide with tremendous anxiety. Remembering how I fell asleep that night and even to this day the memory comes to play; it still have a hair raising affect but it's no more my lord and savior over me.

7.   Lefty says: As I lay there in the bed; I have to honest with me it didn't feel like know dream folks all I know was in this dream state a darkness consumed me to the point I could not breathe. It was like I was in a cocoon of darkness suffocating me, and it scared the shhhhhell out of me too!

8.   Lefty says: At that time I was reading the bible like it was my last day on earth. And so when this happened all I knew was the bible; the thing about

it was I could breathe; it was almost like being suffocated but you only have enough mouth and air space to speak, so I said Jesus, Jesus, by the blood of Jesus. No kidding I kept saying Jesus. It didn't leave right away but it left.

Lefty says: That was an experience I have never had again.

9.   Lefty says: I had one dream, it was more like it was coming from outside, and I was just experiencing what was going on in the outer world which I believe were spirit activities; any way it was in 2002. A very difficult time in my life; I'm a cut right to the point. I was 22 years old at the time and it was very late near midnight before I dosed off to sleep. While I were in my room sleeping on the opposite side of my bed with my left arm hanging off the bed; To this day the memory and the feeling was real as you touching my hand. A part me felt like long finger nails were scratching my skin, not literally cutting and breaking my skin. It felt more like a gentle scratch over the flesh making no visible markings. I got up that morning and looked at my left arm and there wasn't anything there. That shook me up pretty good.

10. Lefty says: I have learned that all spirits living in this flesh jacket or coat needs a foundation solid enough to fend off dark energies, because if you do not have one you will be taken under. Fear is what negative energies feed off, soul what are you going to do with yourselves now?

11. Lefty says: I have really grown since then and have not encountered my evil self, because this day my evil self has been put in one's place and is now walking with me in harmony and not as enemies.

12. Lefty says: I have never shared my experiences to know one; today I have made it official to share me with all of me out there who is still dreaming and do not know how to get out of this prison of darkness. My every word and experiences are true and honest with no thought of doubt; I stand on my every word I have written. I am a living witness to all of my dreams and experiences. All my experiences are not dark energies, my dreams and experiences are also adventurous, loving, and hopeful.

13. Lefty says: Let's prepare ourselves now while living in these bodies to send our spirits back to heaven where it's beautiful and forever in agreement and in harmony.

Lefty says: In 2010 at the age of 30 now. I experienced—again if it were a dream it felt more like it was an outward spiritual influence. We are all spirit but for now we dealing with this flesh as long as we live in these bodies of flesh, what I'm saying is that whatever affects the senses in this realm that is material we are also affected, this is what trigger dreams, outer world activities.

Lefty says: So as I lay there in my bed sleep until my senses sensed a love and a peace while I was a sleep that everything is going to be ok, but the most extraordinary part about it all was that I sensed a hand placed on my heart, such a warming embrace that let me know that I'm not alone

That there is hope, there is love, and there is peace in the mist of confusion and doubt.

These are My Dreams and Experiences."

My Journal, The Book Of Me With Insight

GENDER & RELATIONSHIPS

BOOK THREE, CHAPTER TWELVE

Lefty says: "My relationship first have to be with me before I can even have a nice conversation—or let me say a decent conversation with that person wearing the same flesh made of soil and dirt just like me,

2. Right says: It isn't cool to stay in a reckless game when hate outweighs love and happiness in a so called relationship. One of you has to make a move and get out!

3. Lefty says: If I'm not in harmony, no way can I join hands with another person because the seed I have implanted in me Is a story teller as we all call it.

4.   Lefty says: Woman can get away with so much because she has tapped into her-emotions that make up her effeminate personality; she loses touch though she's her own worst enemy.

5.   Lefty says: <u>Man needs to first find his place in me before entering into outer world relationships with another spirit personality wearing this jacket or coat of flesh we only are here to borrow for a certain amount of time if we don't shorten our days by foolishness and self-hate.</u>

6.   Lefty says: His journey to seek a mate to match his spirit in his out of place condition can cause him to find the same spirit like himself and can either destroy him or purge him to make a change to do better and motivated to clean up his acts of disorder.

7.   Lefty says: Man is never acting alone. He is not all by himself, she plays a major role.

       Right says: I'm saying to you all don't be a wild (out of control) show girl, stay alert and be ready to defend language, soul language keeping in place with the man who's in place.

8.   Lefty says: Man and woman are weak without balance of mind.

9. Right says: Girls! You know I'm seeing me!

   Right says: He likes you!

10. Lefty says: Stand your ground. Don't ever give in to a man if he doesn't lay out his blue print of one's own life and present which is the future plans that is a base that isn't cracked by deep seated hate dictated by an uncontrollable temper.

11. Lefty says: Tempers not under control can blow a fuse in any relationship.

12. Lefty says: Communication doesn't have to be all sophisticated, good solid relationships come from simplicity and honesty.

   Too much intelligence and competition can overcome soulish affection and softness.

13. Right says: Meekness is a requirement in any relationship brothers and sisters!

14. Right says: You know what happens when I'm not involved in this relationship? There is only division, outrage, and emotional disorder as well as spiritual, Amen somebody!

15. Lefty says: When there is no lowliness problems are formed turning slowly into hard knots unable to come apart, but instead it gets tighter and tighter making it even more impossible. Problems are now rooted deep until one day it will soon twist and pop causing a great separation. Even the scripts say, 'Every kingdom divided against itself will be ruined, and every city or household divided against itself will not stand.' Matt 12:25 NIV.

16. Lefty says: I must say that if a man can maintain his (soul) fire in the mist of women and man he will have a higher chance to win other souls to understanding.

17. Lefty says: I alone cannot accomplish what needs to be accomplished without my artist and creativity helping me to put the pieces to the puzzle together.

18. Lefty says: Solving a problem is possible with my help-pure by my side in the mist of doubt.

19. Right says: As long as we still in this body we will experience pain!

20. Right says: Whether you accept me or not there isn't no escaping!

21. Right says: You running from this natural body, and all you doing is running further downhill, scary places you see in them movies you be watching and recording, you do know I'm keeping this movie live in my home beneath that head of yours, seriously!

    You are what cha you eat brothers and sisters.

    So why make it harder on yourselves? Why you planting seeds of doubt?

22. Lefty says: You readers are engaging in relationships and don't even know how to control me; instead you readers rather use me to curse and tell a story (lie) to get what you want, even to the point of murdering me for a taste of money, power, and respect.

23. Right says: Relationships are only going to last if I'm in my place, and happy face is in his.

24. Lefty says: What do you think about me?

    Right says: Man!

25. Lefty says: So it doesn't matter what body I am indwelling. I am man.

26. Lefty says: Man and man characteristics is just that—Man. man is spirit and is formed as man in flesh, so whether you're a women or a man to all of you reading about me that am in you possess man spirit.

27. Lefty says: Now the same goes for the womanish spirit. She is spirit first dwelling in man and women, she is formed and made into flesh; she has always been a helper.

28. Lefty says: I must say that it is better for a man who has found his (other self) weakness then to get into a relationship with a person willing to physically harm him because of lack of trust and insecurity.

29. Right says: Women don't you ever get out of your place and sell your soul because of a man's promises. You better have your own foundation; you better have a root in me that am in you or else you cooking breakfast for a night mare ready to happen!

30. Right says: You might say, 'But I'm getting older!' Well honey, let me say this, that it is better to be drama free then to live the rest of your natural life feeling pressed down and hell bound, you feel me now? If you with me that am in you let us all say, Amen!

31. Right says: Relationships can last forever if you can hold the (Your tongue and mouth) burn in the moment of fires and storms!

32. Lefty says: Man and Women are only manifestations of what we are and that is spiritual energies wearing physical bodies resembling us who are spirit.

31. Lefty says: Telling the truth hurts and can even hurt one's own self if hidden in the heart and mind for a long time.

32. Lefty says: Pain can fade but it can quickly be surfaced with image and word.

33. Right says: That's right! I'm the one playing them movies! So when anytime spokesman is saying you remember? Just remember there is no photo without me! Keep that in mind my brothers and sisters!

34. Lefty says: <u>If you want a relationship with someone first. You have to know me that am in you and know what I possess so I can work honestly with this body in soundness and in happiness while living in this body made of dirt and soil brothers and sisters. You must then know that strength and meekness must work hand and hand to fulfill any goal or mission.</u>

35. Right says: You see how my insight can change lives? This is all it takes, understanding! That's my Job!

36. Right says: All of you reading this hour and moment don't be afraid! Come back to me and live!

37. Lefty says: Joy is mine and together this relationship can never fail.

38. Lefty says: I know you reading have made mistakes in the past and present time, but we forgive you all for your errors.

39. Lefty says: The bible calls them sins, but this very moment I speak to me who am reading I call them errors this day.

40. Lefty says: My language has been change since day one and continues to change because of me that am in you who are reading about me this very moment that you inhale and exhale with both eyes on this page and with every heartbeat.

41. Right says: There is no escaping me! You may escape them physical relationships, but all I'm asking is that you know me. Is that hard to ask?

You find this treasure you are surely on your way to soundness!

42. Lefty says: Physical relationships keep us normal, but if we are not honestly living to grow spiritually you setting yourselves up to falling into worlds of darkness, drama, and deep anguish.

43. Right says: As long as I'm here you will feel my emotional ways!

44. Lefty says: Not all men will be married and in a relationship with a woman; the only personality he will bond with and hold fast too is she beside him.

45. Right says: That's me by the way if you don't know it! Didn't bible say something about . . . ?

    Lefty says: It says in the scripture, Jesus said, "'I tell you that anyone who divorces his wife, except for marital unfaithfulness, and marries another woman commits adultery.

    The disciples said to him, "If this is the situation between a husband and wife, it is better not to marry."

Jesus replied, "Not everyone can accept this word, but only those to whom it has been given. For some are eunuchs because they were born that way; others were made that way by men; and others have renounced marriage because of the kingdom of heaven." Matt 19:9-12 NIV.

46. Lefty says: A man who can live with himself has shown that he hasn't abandoned her who is his neighbor and helper.

47. Lefty says: I am seeing that man has already separated me that am in him, and is also in all of you who are reading this very hour and moment.

48. Lefty says: When a women is out of place she is hell on two feet, and the same goes for man.

49. Lefty says: It's time to prepare and leave this hell on earth now or else you'll be the one left behind.

50. Lefty says: To remain at peace and in soundness of mind and body we must recognize and know our place at all times. To have a good solid relationship you got to know how to control your temper if you want praise and honor.

51. Lefty says: When you remain faithful your mate will find you.

52. Lefty says: It is also a choice to engage in a relationship with the opposite gender.

53. Right says: Opposite Gender! You know you really sound like a Microsoft narrator when you said that!

54. Right says: ladies don't put a side your dreams to please the world! Know me first!

55. Right says: If you want to sing! It's in me!

   If you want to dance! It's in me!

   If you want to be an artist! It's in me!

   Don't deny my love and meekness!

   It's real!

56. Right says: Don't you know brothers and sisters that if I'm not harmonizing it's pretty hard to get a job!

57. Right says: And it doesn't matter how many diplomas and degrees you claiming!

58.   Right says: If I'm not right and in my place it's a real struggle, even if you do find me you still going to struggle! The only difference is you know me!

59.   Right says: I'm closing it down brothers and sisters in a little bit.

60.   Right says: As long as we are harmonizing not anything touching me that is in all of you readers! Even the scripts say: 'And the earth helped the woman, and the earth opened her mouth, and swallowed up the flood which the dragon cast out of his mouth. Revelations 12:16 KJV.

61.   Lefty says: Knowing our place can give me the authority and the confidence with meekness by my side these words without a doubt.

Right says: Without a doubt! Do you here that?

Lefty says: This is beautiful and encouraging to us when the scripture says: 'He that overcometh shall inherit all things; and I will be his (and her) God, and he (and she) shall be my son (and daughter)." Revelations 21:7 KJV.

Closing Remarks

Lefty says: May these words be encouragement to all of me out there who is willing to find understanding, wisdom, help and guidance in these difficult times. The end is not hear as long as you have breath and is still walking these soils, there is hope, for I am a living witness and so can you be a light in the mist of chaos and confusion that is going on around the world. Let us become common and normal human beings to one another and not a problem but instead let's become the solution.

Right says: You hear us brothers and sisters? Let us!

FINAL ACKNOWLEDGEMENT

Scripture quotations taken out of the HOLY BIBLE, Authorized KING JAMES VERSION World Bible Publishers.

Pagepg12 **judges16:15-19 New International version.**
pg18pg. pg 30 Daniel 4:16/28-33 pg977 New International version.

Ephesians pg57 6:12-17 pg1310 New International version.
Pg44proverbs4:5-9 GNT bible pg576 Jeremiah pg69 51:30KJV.
Pg922. Nahum pg70 2:10GNT pg828. Pg70 Psalms 119:120
KJVpg736. Pg72 Habakkuk GNT. pg921 Pg72 Tobit 3:7-10
GNT. Deuterocanonical/Apocrypha pg854 pg96 1 Samuel
18:8-12pg324. NIV. Pg. 97psalms 119:70pg 690. NIVpg97
Genesis 37:19NIV Pg47. pg99 1 peter 5:8 NIV Pg1370. pg100
John 11:33-36 NIV pg. 1193 Pg. 4Genesis 4:4-9 GNT. Pg102
pg105 Genesis 3:6; 12 PPg.3 GNT Pg104 Genesis1:27 pg2.
GNT. Pg106 Genesis 6:5 GNT. Pg5. Pg106 Genesis6:5-7 pg5.
Pg113 psalms77:5-6NIV. pg658. pg127 Pg227 Deuteronomy
28:66 NIV. Pg227. PG201 Proverbs 7:4, 11, 21, 11-23.
Pg649. pg 114 1peter 3:4 GNT. Pg325 Pg114 Ephesians5:28
NIV. Pg1309 Pg1442Chronicles Pg494NIV. Pg144 Numbers
16:32Pg144NIV. Pg. 243 Nehemiah 2:1-2 Pg. 424. Matthew
6:3kjv. Pg350-1004. pg168 Luke 6:21-23GNT.1139pg pg275
luke7:3-9GNT. Pg169 Luke7-36-39; 44, 45, 46, 47, 48; 50.
GNT. Pg1993. Pg170 Corinth2:3 pg247. GNT.

James4:9-10GNT 171-320pg. Luke 19:46 181-114pg 188pg
Luke 16:19-25-31. NLT. 1195pg. Isaiah 44:8 pg196-723pg
GNT. Isaiah 44:21 pg198-723 GNT. Matt 11:29 Pg209-1102
KJV. Matt6:3 210-1094pg KJV. Luk22:3-6 227-117pg
Matt27:3-228-43pg GNT. Job 1:14-19 pg246-525 GNT.
Matt12:25 666-1078pg NIV. Matt19:9-12 273-1088 NIV.
Rev 12:16 276-1445pg KJV. Rev 21:7 276-1453 KJV.